She, Disrupts

A Black Woman's Journey in the STEM and AI Industries

Paulette Watson

Paulette Watson

Disclaimer

The information in this book, is for general information only. Paulette Watson provides the details and while we endeavour to keep the information up to date and correct. I make no representations, or warranties of any kind, expressed or implied, about the completeness, accuracy, reliability, suitability. Including, availability, regarding this publication or the information, products, services, or related graphics in this publication, for any purpose. Any reliance you place on such information is, therefore, is strictly at your own risk. In no event, will we be liable for any loss or damage, including, without limitation, indirect or consequential loss or damage. Or any loss or damage, arising from loss of data or profits, relating to the use of this publication. Through this book, you can link to other resources and contacts, which are not under the control of Paulette Watson. We have no control over the nature, content, and availability of those responsible for their management, operation, or function. Including any links, does not imply a recommendation or endorse the views expressed within them. At the time of writing, we tried to keep the information in this publication current. Paulette Watson is not liable for outdated or unavailable information caused by factors beyond our control.

Contact Paulette Watson at: info@paulettewatson.com

Copyright Year: November 2020, First edition.
Copyright Notice: Published by Paulette Watson. Unless permission is granted by Paulette Watson, no part of this book may be reproduced in any form or by any means.

Results in this copyright notice:

© 2020 Paulette Watson. All rights reserved.

ISBN: 978-1-304-92075-1

She, Disrupts

A Black Woman's Journey in the STEM and AI Industries

Dedication

To my beloved daughter,

We live in a world of endless possibilities, and I dedicate this book to you with a heart full of hope and determination. You inspire me every day with your boundless curiosity and unyielding spirit. I am proud to be your mama. This book is a testament to the legacy we aim to create, not just for you, but for all the young Black women who deserve every chance to succeed.

In a rapidly growing digital landscape, the digital skills gap has become a chasm, and we refuse to stand by and let it widen. Our mission is clear: to raise one million Black women's and girls' aspirations in STEM, AI, and Web 3-related careers. I want to forge a pathway for talented Black women like you to thrive in this digital era. I commit us to closing the digital skills gap, one opportunity at a time.

Our vision reaches far beyond the present as we aspire to democratize this space for a fairer future for all. We believe that by empowering and uplifting Black women, we can create a ripple effect that touches the lives of countless others. Our mission is not just a mission; it is a legacy in the making that will endure for generations.

I dedicate us to leaving a mark, building a bridge over the digital divide, and nurturing a 500-strong legacy of brilliant Black women who will shape the future. This book is a testament to our commitment, a symbol of our unwavering belief in you and the incredible potential of every Black woman.

With all my love and a heart full of dreams for you and for all the daughters of tomorrow.

Paulette Watson

Contents

Acknowledgements 8
About the Author 11
Foreword... 18
Preface 21
Introduction 26
Chapter 1 – The Evolution of STEM in the UK........................ 32
    The Call for STEM... 36
    Disparity of Women in Tech 39
    BAME Women in STEM Statistics... 41
Chapter 2–Politics & STEM.. 53
    Race and Gender in the UK.. 55
    STEM and its Impact on Black Women and Society............... 67
    Black Women in Social Housing 67
    Single Parenting and Health 68
    Impact of Covid-19 on Families 69
    Black Women in Employment... 70
Chapter 3–Race, Gender & Technology................................. 75
    Predictive Software Technology.. 89
    Oppressive Algorithms 91
Chapter 4–STEM, the Economy & Economics in the U.K. & the World.. 95
    STEM's Role in the Economy... 95
    Breaking down, STEM and its broader role: 97

How Important is STEM Concerning the Broader Economy 100

Focus On the Demand for Stem Jobs & Skills in Britain 104

Chapter 5 - How STEM Interacts with the Environment 125

What is Climate Change? 125

How do we educate women and girls to help raise climate change awareness? 127

Fewer Women in Science 129

Why does the #BeMedigitalinclusion program matter for climate science? 131

How will the #BeMedigitalinclusion of female climate change scientists, offer a different perspective? 134

What the future looks like for STEM in the Environment? .. 136

Chapter 6–Case Studies 139

Chapter 7–COVID-19 168

Chapter 8 - Overview: GHANA 173

Gender Context: 177

Education: 177

Teacher Training: 177

Chapter 9 - Overview: UNITED STATES 184

Education Attainment Gaps 184

Wealth 185

Health 189

Pay 189

Mental Health 190

Chapter 10 - What is AI? 194

Round Up 208

REFERENCES 212

Acknowledgements

It has been a journey, but I did it. Despite the challenges, I am incredibly grateful for the support and love I have received along the way. This book would not have been possible without the unwavering support of some remarkable individuals.

First, I have to give God thanks for keeping me through this journey. If it wasn't for him, I never would have made it. I dedicated this book to my beloved daughter, Sym. Your love and care have been my driving force and my source of inspiration. You have filled my life with endless joy and purpose, and it is for you. I have poured my heart and soul into these pages. May this book serve as a testament to the love between a parent and a child. You rock, baby girl–*mama loves you*.

I would like to express my heartfelt gratitude to Kofi. Your unwavering support, encouragement, and belief in me throughout the process of writing this book has been my anchor. Your support and hard work were essential for making this project successful. I am forever grateful for your unwavering presence in my life.

I also want to extend my gratitude to my sisters, Rose, and Charly, whose support and dedication helped in the making of this book. We spent many hours discussing and refining the ideas in these pages, and it was both productive and fun. Your unwavering belief in my work kept me going, and I am blessed to have you both by my side.

To Kwame, my mentor, you have been exceptional, your patience, your support has been priceless–thank you.

To all the women and girls, who took time out of their busy lives to attend my speeches, workshops, and talks, I am profoundly grateful. Your engagement, enthusiasm, and feedback have shaped the content of this book. It is my hope, that the words on these pages empower and inspire you in return. Together, we can continue to create positive change in our world.

To all my allies who have been there for me from day dot, a big "Thank You".

Last, but certainly not least, I want to acknowledge parents everywhere. Your dedication to supporting and guiding your children is the basis for the next generation. Your dedication to supporting and guiding your children is the basis for the next generation. This book is a tribute to the countless parents who strive every day to provide the best possible future for their children. Your sacrifices and love are the driving force behind my commitment to making this world a better place for the generations to come. Although Dad, you are not here anymore; I am still grateful to you for believing in my dream. Mum, my Queen, my everything–you mean the world to me–I love you so much–my best friend.

In closing, I am humbled by the collective efforts and love that have gone into the creation of this book. I hope these words resonate with readers from all walks of life, inspiring positive change and fostering a brighter future for us all.

It will also include us in the 4th digital revolution and create opportunities for all.

About the Author

Paulette Watson is creating a pipeline of Black women's talent by bridging the Digital Divide for Black women in Tech.

Paulette is a passionate tech advocate, dedicated to closing the digital skills gap and empowering Black women in the technology sector. Together, with her unwavering commitment to diversity, equity, and inclusion. Paulette is a driving force for diversity and inclusion in the digital world, giving underrepresented voices a powerful platform. She is unapologetic in her approach and does everything to ensure that it does not leave Black women behind.

Early Life and Education

Born into a family that encouraged curiosity and learning, Paulette's journey into the tech industry began at a young age. Growing up in a culturally rich and diverse community, she quickly recognized the disparities in access to technology and digital education. Determined to make a difference, she embarked on a path of academic excellence. Paulette Watson understands the need for quality education for children and young people (C.Y.P.) from all backgrounds. As the head of Academy Achievers, she advocates for high-quality support in schools. With roles as a computer science teacher, E-learning Head, and ICT Director. She devoted almost 12 years to working with students from disadvantaged backgrounds. Paulette analyses the mental inequality in science, technology, engineering, and maths (STEM) using her community projects. Exploring the real-life experiences of children and young people's biased treatment from the school system (exclusions) and the Police (especially now that A.I. facial recognition has severe biases). Paulette understands how to examine mental inequality in education and develops a digital roadmap to include children and young people. Her skills and experiences range from Business, Technology, and Data Sciences; her key interests are in: *Education, Health, Agriculture, FinTech, Climate Change, ESG, Social Mobility, Diversity & Inclusion.* Including how 'Technology' can have a positive or negative impact on

Black women in 'Big *Data, AI, Algorithms, Data Structures, IoT, Blockchain, Genomics, and Web 3'*.

Black women lack financial investment, quality education, social human capital, and lack of access to network opportunities for these Tech jobs, leading to the digital skills gap.

Paulette Watson has spent a decade as an Educational Technologist, Entrepreneur, Founder and Managing Director. She handled all aspects of the company's communications capabilities that drive the performance of the business. So, from these abilities, she focused on communication and Digital Transformational Strategy, Data Analytics. Including Gender Diversity, and Recruiting, skills that she has applied in the local and global community of Academy Achievers. During the years, Paulette Watson has implemented these values in the Academy's management so staff, local, and international community leaders, parents, children, and young people would be digitally literate and level up for the future of work.

Paulette has two master's degrees, one in Information Computer Technology and International Business Leadership, from a prestigious university, where she excelled academically and engaged in advocacy for marginalized communities on campus. She understood that her educational journey was a stepping stone to creating meaningful change in the tech industry.

Career as a Tech Advocate

Paulette's career took off, as she landed her first job at a renowned tech company. However, she soon realized that her workplace's lack of diversity and representation mirrored the broader tech industry's challenges. This experience ignited her passion for advocacy and the urgent need to address the digital skills gap for Black women.

Driven by her mission, Paulette took on a pivotal role as a global tech advocate for Black women. She started and led the Global #BeMedigitalinclusion initiatives to promote equal opportunities in technology. She is training the next generation of diverse talent, intending to onboard one million global majority women and girls to

STEM, AI, and Web 3. Paulette doesn't just believe in an equal, democratized, and decentralized future; Paulette and her team are actively building it.

Right now, with the #BeMedigitalinclusion WhatsApp and Discord group, the #BeMedigitalinclusion young women can join themed communities that resonate with them and have conversations on topics they may have previously hesitated to discuss, owing to stigma and fear of harassment. The best thing about Web 3, is the principle of participative ownership; our members can create content, invite other women, and be equal owners in what they make together.

Paulette has sat on several boards: EqualiTeam in Lewisham, as Treasurer and Vice-Chair, and Youth First as Non-Executive Director. Run by a collectively owned group of professional youth workers and young people. A new member of the Newham Governors' Forum Association, which is affiliated with the National Governance Association. She also served on the Local School Board, as a co-opted governor at Cumberland Trust Secondary School. She has attended the

"International Visitors Leadership Program" organized by the United States Department, United States Department of Defense or State. Places she visited: Federalism at the Meridian International Center, Fulbright Teacher Exchange Program, National Council on US-Arab Relations, Gallop Poll, Capital Communications Group, United States Department of Defense, United States Department of State, Democratic National Committee, Capitol Hill. The Supreme Court of the United States, US House of Representatives, Center for Strategic & International Studies, Maryland General Assembly and the Embassy of the United Kingdom; Atlantic Council of the United States, as part of a delegation of the European Union.

Paulette has been Associate Dean at Leysin International School in Switzerland, leading on digital transformation program in partnership with Google. She is now leading the #BeMedigitalinclusion campaign to raise one million global majority of women's and girls' aspirations in Science, Technology, Engineering, and maths-related careers. Her passion is aligning the

#BeMedigitalinclusion goals to the United Nations (U.N.) sustainable development goals: **Education** #4 Quality Education: **Entrepreneurialism** #8 Decent work and economic growth: **Innovation** #9 Industry, Innovation, and Infrastructure: **Social Inclusion** #10 Reduced Inequalities.

Paulette is one of the 100 Global Women and an Ambassador for Mission Impact in Web 3 and Metaverse. In addition, Paulette is also a G100 Engineering Global Advisor Council member for Digital and Technology and Web 3. She will showcase the #BeMedigitalinclusion program in the Mission project to raise one million global majority women and girls' aspirations in STEM and Web 3-related careers across the globe.

Foreword

I am thrilled to write the foreword for this book. Paulette is passionate about closing the digital skills gap for Black women and is one of the most driven people I know.

The digital divide is a major challenge facing our society. Millions of people lack the basic digital skills they need to fully take part in the workforce and society. This gap is especially pronounced among Black women and other marginalized groups and can have a devastating impact on people's lives. It can limit their career opportunities, and ability to access government services, notwithstanding their ability to stay connected with family and friends.

That's why it is so important to support women who are passionate about removing this critical barrier to success. This book is a valuable resource for these women. It provides practical advice and inspiration on how to make a difference.

The author of this book is a Black woman who has overcome significant challenges to become a successful award-winning, leader in the tech industry. She is passionate about helping other Black women succeed in tech.

Paulette shares her own story on the challenges and barriers into tech. It is an essential read for any woman who shares her passion and is also a valuable resource for anyone who wants to make a difference in the lives of Black women. To help them succeed in the tech industry.

This book is well-written and informative, providing practical advice on how to address the digital divide and develop the digital skills needed for a successful career in tech. I commend it to all women, taking inspiration from its narrative, to get involved in the effort to close the digital skills gap for Black women. Together, we can create a more inclusive tech industry and a fairer society.

Mark

Paulette Watson

Mark Stevens is based in the UK and a veteran of forty-three years, in the high-tech, telecommunications, and electronics industry. In the last thirteen years, he has successfully led Ciena's CSR, Sustainability Programs. As well as architecting the leading edge, Community Engagement, and Digital Inclusion programs. He recently established his own sustainability consulting company, having left the position of Director, Sustainability Strategy, Operations, and reporting at Ciena Corporation, after 13 years. Mark has held senior positions in customer satisfaction, quality, and design organizations. Including, manufacturing, services, and customer facing domains. He has also led international integration programs and held senior roles in marketing. One of his successful passions, as a trustee of the charity 'Kids Out UK' is to bring fun and happiness to children, in refuges, who have been victims of domestic violence. Mark is a keen David Bowie fan, and he enjoys jazz music, blowing his own trumpet, classic cars, creative art, in many forms and cruising the oceans.

Preface

Black women and girls are underrepresented in the STEM fields. In 2019, only 28% of the STEM workforce was female, and only 3% of that workforce was Black. This digital skill gap has several negative consequences, both for Black women and girls themselves and for society. Black women and girls are less likely to have access to high-quality education in STEM fields and are more likely to face discrimination and harassment in the workplace. As a result, they are less likely to be hired for STEM jobs, and they are more likely to leave STEM jobs early.

The lack of Black women in STEM fields has several negative consequences for society:

1. It deprives us of the talent and creativity of Black women.
2. It leads to a need for more diversity in the STEM workforce, stifling innovation and creativity.

3. It perpetuates the cycle of poverty and inequality, as Black women and girls are less likely to access high-paying jobs in STEM fields.

We can do so many things to close the digital skill gap for Black women. First, we '*must*' ensure that all Black women and girls have access to high-quality education in STEM fields. We must invest in STEM education, especially in underserved communities, and provide Black women and girls with the resources they need to succeed in STEM.

Secondly, we must create a more inclusive workplace for Black women in STEM fields. It means, addressing discrimination and harassment and creating a workplace culture that is welcoming and supportive of Black women.

Thirdly, we must celebrate the Black women already working in the STEM fields. It will help to inspire other Black women and girls to pursue STEM careers.

Challenges in health, education, housing

Black women face many challenges in health, education, and housing. These difficulties, contribute to the digital skills gap, making it more difficult for Black women, to access the resources and support they need, to succeed in STEM.

Health

The chronic rate of disease, such as, strokes, diabetes, and cancer, is higher among Black women, compared to white women. They, encounter problems such as maternal and infant mortality, racism, poverty, and insufficient healthcare access.

Education

Black girls have a harder time enrolling in advanced Maths and Science courses, in high school, limiting their college opportunities compared to white women. This is because of several factors, including racism, poverty, and a lack of access to quality education.

Housing

Black women are more than likely, to live in poverty than white women. They live in inner city areas, and this is due to the number of factors contributing to this discrimination, which include racism, redlining, and gentrification.

What government and research can do?

The government and research can do so much to help close the digital skill gap for Black women.

Government

The government can invest in STEM education in underserved communities. However, must ensure that all Black women and girls have access to the resources and support needed to succeed in STEM.

The government can also provide Black women and girls with scholarships and grants to help them afford to attend college and pursue STEM degrees.

The government can also invest and collaborate with programs, like the Global #BeMedigitalinclusion. To help Black women transition into STEM careers. Our intention for change would include developing job training, mentorship programs, networking and collaborating with the Global #BeMedigitalinclusion of Sustainable Tech career opportunities.

Research

Research can identify the specific challenges that Black women face in STEM fields. They can develop it further with targeted interventions to address these challenges. The research can develop 'best practices' for recruiting, keeping and promoting Black women in STEM fields.

Conclusion

The digital skill gap for Black women is a complex problem, with no simple solutions. However, to address this issue, the government, researchers, and the private sector all have a role in closing the digital skill gap for Black women. By working together, we can create a more inclusive and fairer STEM workforce that reflects the diversity of our society.

Introduction

I have often shared my story regarding my passion for 'Science and Technology.' I loved learning about the world and building things with my hands, and as a young child, you fear nothing. But as I got older, I realized many barriers stood in my way of pursuing a career in STEM (Science, Technology, Engineering, and Mathematics). One of my biggest challenges was the need for more diversity in STEM fields. Unfortunately, I did not see any role models that looked like me in my science and maths classes, and I regularly felt like I didn't belong. I wouldn't say that I liked school, and never felt motivated to take part in any activities or saw myself as a successful scientist or engineer.

Not only that, but I also faced another challenge-the digital skills gap. In today's world, solid digital skills are critical more than ever, and many people. In particular, those from marginalized communities, require more resources and training, to develop these skills. Making it difficult to vie for jobs in STEM fields, which are increasingly demanding digital skills.

Despite my contentions, I was determined to pursue my passion for STEM. I worked hard, and with my perseverance, I got accepted into a STEM program. But even once I got to college and university, I still faced challenges. I often felt like I was the only one who didn't fit in, and I had to work twice as hard to prove myself. But I kept going; I work as a software engineer and also taught computer science and then started my business to empower women and girls in STEM, AI, and Web 3. I'm grateful for the opportunities I've had, but I know that I'm one of the lucky ones. Many other Black women are passionate about STEM but face many barriers to success.

This book is my account of the challenges I faced as a Black woman pursuing a career in STEM. By sharing my story, I hope I can inspire other Black women to follow their dreams and persevere in adversity.

The Evolution of STEM in the UK

STEM education and research in the UK, has a long and distinguished history. In the 17th century, Sir Isaac Newton made ground-breaking discoveries in physics and mathematics.

The Industrial Revolution led to the development of new technologies and industries, such as steam power and railroads. In the 19th century, the UK was at the forefront of the scientific revolution. Charles Darwin published his theory of evolution, and Louis Pasteur developed the germ theory of disease. The UK continues to be a leader in the 20th century, toward STEM research, with scientists, such as Alan Turing and Stephen Hawking, making significant contributions to their fields.

Britain is still a significant player in the global STEM landscape and has a solid research base, with world-renowned universities, such as Oxford, Cambridge, and Imperial College London. It is, also, home to many successful tech companies, such as ARM Holdings, Google DeepMind, and Skyscanner.

Politics and STEM

The UK government has long recognized the importance of STEM education, and research on the country's economy in society. In recent years, the government has given resources to STEM education and research, launching several initiatives to promote diversity in STEM fields. As they recognize the importance of the government's industrial strategy, which identifies STEM as a crucial sector of the UK economy. So, a few programs have been initiated, to encourage more women and girls to pursue careers in STEM - '*STEM Ambassadors Program and the WISE Campaign*'.

Despite the government's investment in STEM, challenges still need to be addressed, because the UK has a relatively low proportion of women, Black, and ethnic minorities, in STEM fields. Furthermore, it needs to do more to ensure everyone has access to the digital skills necessary to succeed in the modern economy.

Race, Gender, and Tech

There is an ever-growing awareness, of the importance of diversity in tech. As a diverse workforce, brings with it, a variety of perspectives and experiences, which can lead to better decision-making and more innovative products and services. However, there is still a significant under-representation of women, Black, and ethnic minorities in tech. In the case of the UK. Women comprise only 22% of the tech workforce, and Black and ethnic minorities make up only 17%. The factors are; under-representation and the need for more role models. Many young women, from Black and ethnic minorities, don't see themselves represented in the tech industry, so they believe it is not a viable career path for them. Notwithstanding, the need for more access to opportunities. Young women from Black and ethnic minorities are also less likely, to have access to the resources and training they require, helping to develop their skills for a tech career.

She, Disrupts

Finally, there is the question of discrimination!

And I am happy to present to you–**SHE DISRUPTS!**

Chapter 1 – The Evolution of STEM in the UK

"Engineering is a successful profession". There is the satisfaction of watching a figment of the imagination emerge through the aid of science to a plan on paper. Then it moves to realization in stone, metal, or energy. Then it brings homes to men or women. Therefore, it elevates the standard of living and adds to the comforts of life. This is the engineer's high privilege." Herbert Hoover, 31st President of the USA.

As a child growing up in the early 1980s, I remember the era of modern technology, and the launch of the personal computer. This was fun and exciting, and I loved going to school and entering the computer labs. While at home, I had my personal computer that I played with at every opportunity. I was addicted to the Pac-Man and Tetris games and now, forty years later, things have changed dramatically. You cannot leave your home without a smart phone, as the advancement of technology increases. Such is our growing dependency on these new and emerging skills, such as A. I Machine learning, the Internet of Things and Blockchain. Our economy now reflects the growing dependency on technology-based businesses.

It is also clear that the Covid-19 global pandemic has hit our community hard. The forecast is still unclear and understood, regarding the long-term impact of the last eighteen months upon the economy, employment, and health of our community. There is a desperate need for economic growth, job creation, and innovation that can positively improve people's daily lives, the tech ecosystem provides many opportunities. I am convinced that we will preside over a critical period in the history of UK tech, where we will see technology lead, in driving the economy's recovery. We will also see our community reconnect its relationship with the Caribbean, Africa, Europe, and other international partners. The hard questions I am asking are about the future of work. Issues relating to diversity and inclusion, and a fair opportunity for all. Technology is changing quickly around us, and our real challenge is to equip our workforce with STEM qualifications. If we are to sustain growth, in our economy. That is why, it is so important to understand science, technology, engineering, maths (STEM) and the reason, it is, such a big issue with our community and in particular, for the global majority of women and girls.

What is STEM?

The acronym STEM stands for science, technology, engineering, and maths. These subjects are interrelated and can be used, interchangeably, by direct guidance. Here is a definition of STEM, that I have set, within three main points.

(1) STEM in education builds a foundation for maths and science in pre-school, which is further developed in primary and post-primary education. These children and young people, in the post primary sector, are engaged in studying mathematics up to the age of 16. Although, they seek to choose from a variety of inter-related science/technology courses. They provide the students, not only, with knowledge of the subjects. But, also to develop investigative and problem-solving skills, with an understanding of, their application in the real world, and impact on the society. From post-16 through to tertiary level, they offer young people a wide portfolio of qualifications to meet their personal aspirations.

(2) STEM, in society, is concerned with equipping the public with sufficient knowledge and understanding of issues relating to STEM. So, they can then make informed judgments about the many technological challenges facing them. Understanding the contribution of STEM in everyday life and its impact on the economy through a vibrant private sector that offers rewarding career opportunities for young people. We need to ensure that they are, digitally equipped and prepared to take on the 21st century. Society needs to be well-informed of the uses of new technologies and the accompanying ethical and moral issues. Then we face consulting and engaging in an informed environment, the challenge of making life decisions on new and

emerging technological issues, such as, environmental, social governance (ESG) and climate change, together with globalization.

(3) STEM in the economy, is concerned with having enough people with the digital skills and knowledge required to grow STEM based businesses. Leading to future economic growth and prosperity. STEM plays a significant role in our lives now, more than ever, since technology enables digital connectivity.

The Call for STEM

Equal access to education is a human right, and this applies to STEM subjects too. This, however, has not always been the case. Currently, one will find a gender gap, with UNESCO reporting that women make up less than 30% of the world's researchers. This under-representation occurs in every region of the world. Boys have traditionally been more likely to choose STEM subjects, and go into further and higher education, to study for STEM degrees at university.

Something needs to be done to close this gap. We need more girls to study STEM subjects. We need to address this issue head on, by tackling the stereotypical views that they expose us to, on a regular basis. They reflect these beliefs in the under-represented STEM occupations. Specifically, making up 14.4%[1] working in STEM in the UK. Despite being about half of the workforce. This is a big issue, because we are well short of the UK's goal, of reaching a mass of 30%. Therefore, it is critical that we increase the number of women in STEM, as it will increase the UK's labour value by, at least, £2bn[2].

In the UK, over the last few years, it has seen a 31% increase in the number of women and girls taking up STEM subjects. Also, an *increase in the number of young women taking Mathematics and Further Mathematics*, <u>by around 2.8% and 3.9%</u>, respectively.[3] This picture is looking promising for women in STEM. Between 2011 and 2020 *the number of women accepted on to full-time STEM undergraduate courses, increased by 50.1% in the UK*. Within the same period, the proportion of women entering full-time undergraduate courses taking

STEM subjects increased from 33.6% to 41.4%.[45] Overall, the numbers of students studying science, technology, engineering, and mathematics (STEM) is rising. Yet, the evidence shows that tech employers are not meeting the demand for higher-level STEM skills. This is a major issue, especially in the manufacturing, construction, engineering, science, and technology sectors. Therefore, the addition of apprenticeships, these high-level skills jobs can be accessed, and will address the STEM gender imbalance by supporting more women into these positions.

Currently, the harsh reality in London sees only, 3% of the technology industry employees are Black. According, to data compiled for the Evening Standard[6], by Tech Nation, a grand total of 15% come from Black, Asian, and Minority Ethnic (BAME) backgrounds[7]. More needs to be done to diversify the tech sector and to ensure that the next generation of talent can feel empowered, to be digitally equipped to apply for tech careers. The data is disappointing, since Black people only make up 13% of the London population. Therefore, it is clear that there is a diversity of issues within the Tech industry. Personally, I was unaware of this issue, until I was at the WinTrade Global business seminar 2019 and listened to Alison Rose[8] talk about her review called *Alison Rose. A review of Female Entrepreneurship and* referred to *The Burt Report: Inclusive Support for Women in Enterprise, 2015*. Citing that women represented less than 25% of business in the UK's five most productive companies. Wherein, one-woman board members outperformed those without women, by 26% and over. While listening to her, I thought how shocking the data was and curious to find out what the story was behind Black Women in the industry. In my conclusion of the situation, I anticipated it would be a challenge, given the disproportionate lack of opportunity, that most of the women experience, while trying to get into the STEM industry.

Disparity of Women in Tech

According to my analysis, *the experiences of Black Women in the Information Technology Industry.*[9] Although, there have been attempts made to get more Black women in Tech. We still have a long way to go.

According to the British Computer Society (BCS), the Chartered Institute for Information Technology. Now, more than ever, women are working in Information Technology roles across the UK (at the last count, there were 326,000 in total). Making up a record share of 20% in the specialist Information Technology (IT) workforce. According to Rashik Parmar CEO, BCS, states that through the BCS Women Specialist Groups, there has been a slight improvement, in that women now account for 23% of the IT workforce, against a steady 17%, in previous years. We can see some progress, but more needs to be done.

Women in Tech

In 2019, only an average of 9% of BAME of IT specialists were at Director Level and 32% of BAME IT specialists were managers or team leaders, compared to 43% of white IT professionals. The average female representation of the FTSE 100 board is 33%[10].

BAME Women in STEM Statistics

Black and ethnic minority workers make up 12% of the UK workforce[11,12]. The employment rate for Ethnic Minorities in the UK is only 62.8% compared with an employment rate for white workers of 75.6%, according to, McGregor-Smith Review[13]. Another point to addressing gender diversity, is The Black British Professionals in STEM (BBSTEM)[14], where it is made clear, that just 6.2% of UK domicile students enrolled onto STEM-related subjects at UK universities are Black (4.8% Black African, 1.2% Black Caribbean, 0.2% Black Other).

When we look at figures for high-level employees, the representation of BAME women, is extremely worrying, within the top tech firms in the UK. As over 70% of boards and senior executive teams, do not have a BAME member; in fact, women of BAME backgrounds only make up around 2% of boards and senior executive teams. When looking into secondary data, from the Office of National Statistics (ONS) Labour Force Survey, BCS. The Chartered Institute for IT[15] found in 2019 that the 249,000 women working in UK technology accounted for 17% of IT specialists in the region. A figure which has only grown by 1% over the past five years. There is a record number of women in IT, with Black women still being underrepresented[16].

In the same year, there were 268,000 Black, Asian, and minority ethnic (BAME) IT specialists in the UK, accounting for 18% of IT workers. A number that has increased by 2% over the past five years from 16% in to 2015. Indian IT specialists account for 8% of the total, while Black African/Caribbean or Black British and Pakistani or Bangladeshi backgrounds each represent 2%[17].

BAME Women in Tech

The percentage of Black women in IT positions increased from 0.3% in 2019 to 0.7% in 2020, According to British Computer Society (BCS), based on ONS data[18]. However, Black women are still severely underrepresented in IT and, by comparison, across other, occupations[19] their level of representation, is 2.5

times higher. As a whole, there were 31,000 Black people working in IT positions, across the UK in the second quarter of the year – 1.9% of the total IT specialist workforce[20].

Unfortunately, this disparity in the Tech Industry is not exclusive to the UK. According to the United Nations Educational Science and Cultural Organization (UNESCO) only 23% of STEM[21,22] talent globally, is female. It mirrored this disparity in the tech industry, in South Africa. The current data[23] shows that there is a "leaky pipeline" leading to a few women in STEM careers. In South Africa, 50.3% of girls compared to 58.6% of boys achieved 30% or higher in Mathematics in the National Senior Certificate Examination. In the Eswatini General Certificate of Secondary Education, 22% of girls achieved a pass grade in Mathematics, compared to 35% of boys. Whereas the corresponding figures in science were 24% for girls and 31% for boys.

The same is true in corporate leadership and executive positions in desperate need of female representation. As old-fashioned stereotypes, gender bias, and under-representation continue to be a worldwide challenge. Girls in South Africa, Kenya, Portugal, and Latvia are being *encouraged in STEM fields with role models, mentoring programs, and career opportunities*. An example is in Portugal, where its booming start-up scene is now one of the best places to work across the European Union for women in technology.

As explained by the technology job platform - Honey Pot, Portugal[24] has the smallest difference between the gender pay gap in the tech industry and the overall gender pay gap in the National Economy. This makes choosing a career in technology economically less risky for women in Portugal than it would be in other countries. According to Eurostat data,[25] Latvia has the highest figure - 53% - in Europe of women managers. Also, the start-up scene is also matriarchal with the leading players - Tech chill, Tech hub Riga, and the Latvian Startup Association - all headed by women. The research abroad in Africa and Europe will help to explore what strategies they have put in place for women, what lessons they can learn, and what works well.

Black Girls in Technology

There is a deeper problem here with Black girls being digitally excluded. The #BeMedigitalinclusion programmes aim to raise the aspiration of one million global majority women and girls in Science, Technology, Engineering, Maths and related careers. Currently[26]:

- Black people make up 13% of the population in London;
- In London, only 3% of the technology industry's employees are Black;
- A grand total of 15% come from BAME backgrounds (compared to other ethnic groups) according to Tech Nation.

Writing this story is painful, but it's so authentic in so many ways. I know the majority of Black women and girls will relate in some way to one another. So, I will briefly discuss the following:

Lack of early educational investment

Exclusion rates amongst young people is high! Later in the book, I talk about other challenges that Black women face, on a daily basis. I remember as a child; I could read and write from the age of 5 years. My foundation was good, and this is the case for many Black Afro-Caribbean children too. Something happened when we entered the British education system. I disliked school, the building, the teachers, and the curriculum was very dull, narrow, and dry. On reflection, I can fully understand the barriers to education equity, which include disproportionate poverty. This type of poverty remains one of the most significant moral dilemmas our community faces daily. It seems as if they instituted a deliberate system to make it difficult for Black people to achieve upward mobility.

Why do I say this?

In my role as Director of E-learning and Computer Science, it was my responsibility to design and implement the curriculum and program of study. I was the one who chose which fun topics to do for each year. We did (Scratch, Python, HTML, Graphics, Multimedia, Gaming, and Networks Hardware (Cisco) - this was based on having a relationship with the students and using emotional and social intelligence to thoroughly understand what would work and what wouldn't. As the principal moderator for ICT | Computing for Edexcel | AQA and OCR. I attended training and marked GCSE/ A Level papers, during the summer term. I also remember the only information I had was from the school, and the names of the students were anonymized. Likewise, I could look up the school and find out the demographics of the young people. The secondary school that I attended did not have a teacher that looked like me. In fact, most of them were, honestly, half dead - I'm being so serious. There were a high percentage of BAME students, and most of my friends came from single-parent families and received FSM. I did not realize, at the time, that this was a hint of the poverty levels in our borough. Interestingly, according to the educational outcomes of Black pupils,[27] of those eligible for free school meals (FSM). They attained better, on some key measures, than white pupils eligible for FSM. We are more likely to go on to higher education than average, but less likely to achieve top grades, or enter *'prestigious'* universities, and end up in a *'highly skilled'* job. On top of, further study or have career satisfaction. I mean, can you not see, that there is a problem here?

I have also been a member of the local authorities' local wards' committee for Children and Young People, and I have been able to see how policies have been established locally. In addition to that, I have been an opted school governor link lead, for safeguarding children. Having played these roles, I'm thinking, who was representing me back in the 1980s? What were their views on Black children and young people? I remember a few years ago, and as a Director of NPW, they invited me to a retirement party. Ironically, the people that actually came out from the wood works, were old white men - Key leaders and players, within our local education board. I was like, "*really*" these people are having a lovely retirement experience. While most of my friends were living in misery. The GCSE results were poor, and there were no opportunities. Our career options sessions encouraged us to work for Woolworths, which I may add - no longer exists. I also remember, in our schools; the Black boys had a hard time trying to integrate into school life and the senior leadership team, made it a real challenge. Most of our male friends were excluded for silly reasons, and as time went by, and in my role as a member of the Newham Independent Advisory Group. I realized that most Black boys were unfairly treated by police officers, too. However, that is another story for another time. Interestingly, we now have more Black females being excluded and sexually exploited, on account of gang culture, within our communities.

So, the odds are against us!

Schools, and examining boards, have been failing us for decades. Our local authority fails because it is made up of people, who don't even live in the borough, however, make policies, that have a direct impact on us. Representation matters in STEM, because our entire community is governed by it.

Paulette Watson

Case Study

Anna* is 15 years old and has been in the top set of Maths, Triple Science, Computer Science, Art, Music, History, and Geography. She lives with her single parent mother, three siblings, all under the age of six, and live in temporary accommodation.

Her father had been in prison, since she was a baby, because he failed to pay a bill on time, and as a result, he lost his job and home, which led to mental health challenges. Her mother had her at a very young age, with no real family support or network system in place. Unfortunately, for Anna, she did not have the right access to local authority services and because of this, had no choice, but to get on with life. The impact led her to experience mental health challenges, too. At school and in her class, she was the only Black child, and struggled in being accepted in group lessons or creating any friendship groups. Her hair was also an issue, because whenever she left it out, her Head of Year, would constantly tell her, it was unkempt or needed to be tied back. However, Anna was very smart, and at the top of all her subjects. There were no proper opportunities for her to develop her knowledge, because she had family commitments. This landed her in constant trouble, for being late and not completing her homework. Her school did not take into consideration her daily needs, nor provided any pastoral support. Anna lived in poverty, whereby, her mother could barely feed or clothe her and her siblings. Although, she enjoyed Maths and the Sciences, her mother could not afford to send Anna on any residential or field trips. In terms of option month, Anna could not pick the right subjects, since she had no work experience, plus her mum was admitted into hospital, so she had no choice, but to care for her siblings. This cycle of unfortunate events led Anna to dislike school and stop pursuing her studies. Nobody provided her with role models and encouragement, to follow her love for Maths, Sciences, and Computing. On her own journey, she became a single parent, living in a one-bedroom, temporary flat. Unfortunately, she was seeing, history repeating itself, for her young child.

Not her real name

#BeMedigitalinclusion Girls in class: Year 10, Bonus Pastor Secondary School

#BeMedigitalinclusion: Girls from Cumberland Secondary school visit Colt

Chapter 2–Politics & STEM

According to a new report from the World Economic Forum (WEF) called, "The Future of Jobs 2018" machines and algorithms in the workplace are expected to create 133 new roles but will cause 75 million jobs to be displaced by 2022. The report highlights that artificial intelligence could create 58 million net new jobs in the next few years. So even though so many jobs will long be gone, the new roles will see a major shift in quality, location, and permanency of roles. Resulting in businesses expanding, the use of contractors doing specialized work, and the increased use of remote working.

Since the Covid-19 pandemic began, our world has become more complex, volatile, and uncertain. Education is key in setting up our children and young people for a future of intricate challenges. Such as globalization, digitization, and climate change. It is essential that our children and young people (CYP) have access to knowledge of information, understanding the relevant scientific and technical iterations.

Also, the skills needed, such as creative problem-solving, ability to innovate and critical thinking. Known as '21st Century Skills' are significant during this digital transformation process.

In the United Nations Commission on Science and Technology for Development report, - The UN highlights the critical role of science, technology, and innovation in achieving the SDGs. It acknowledged that many technological and development gaps still endure. Globally, in the ODI's report, reducing gender inequalities in science, technology, engineering, and maths. The gender gap highlights the existing Digital and Science, Technology, Engineering and Maths (STEM) divide and recommends key policies for countries and the international community on how to make progress in closing the related gender gaps. The UN's Development Programme Sustainable Development goals, stresses the need to ensure equality and full participation for women in science, in decision-making and sustainable programs.

Race and Gender in the UK

We, fundamentally, need to understand how political decisions can affect the representation and inclusions of Black women in STEM. Whilst the nature of this under-representation varies according to the group and settings. The reasons it exists are complex, and the overall picture is clear. Under-representation is present in many STEM settings, from classrooms to research facilities and boardrooms. So rather than deal with these factors single-handedly, we need to adopt a systemic solutionist approach. Katherine Mathieson, then Chief executive of the British Science Association, argued that under-representation was systemic, and present at all levels and society wide. It was very challenging for single policies or interventions to make a significant difference. She also said the limitation of good intentions was apparent.[28,29]

The global pandemic has hit London hard and is still in a confused state of the long-term impact of the last eighteen months. On the economy, employment, and health of the city. The impact of Brexit, points to the ongoing anxiety around the skills gap, and the threat it poses, to the UK's ability to attract global talent.

Although, the access to STEM for young women and girls, is a global problem. There are disparities amongst race and gender in the United Kingdom and in major cities like London, in particular. There are quite a few key issues that can explain this.[30]

The pandemic has had a ripple impact on women and especially those in leadership roles, where it has wiped out, one to two years of progress across multiple industries. That being so, the gender gap is more likely in sectors that require disruptive technical skills, where women have low representation. For example, in Cloud Computing, women make up 14% of the workforce; in Engineering, 20%; and in Data and AI, 32%. My genuine concerns here are, really, that these new and emerging tech jobs are roles for a tomorrow's world. Yet still, there is, an alarming percentage of women that have barely increased since 2018. We need to ensure that our #BeMedigitalinclusion women and girls have a voice and are exposed to the technology opportunities that are being created, not only improve efficiency, but to improve quality of life. It is clear that, Covid-19 will increase the need for automation and digitization, within the near future.

If the entire population of Black people in London is 13% and there is a problem of diversity in London. As out of 50% of Black and Minority Ethnic (BME) students in universities, approximately, only 5% of them enter the tech industry. In London, only 3% of the technology industry's employees are Black and 15% come from BAME backgrounds. According to Tech Nation, there is also gender and diversity imbalance and the Institute of Coding shows this, in their campaign, _Ctrl The Future. Despite decades of progress towards equality, women remain underrepresented in the UK's technology workforce. As explained by Wise[31], just 23% of the people in STEM roles across the UK are female - and only 5% of leadership positions in the technology are held by women[32]. What's concerning here, is the imbalance does not appear likely to redress in the immediate future: tech opportunities seem to favour men, with women, accounting for just 15.8% of the UK's current generation of engineering and technology undergraduates[33].

According to the PWC global CEO. UK CEOs find it difficult to hire digitally skilled individuals[34], while US CEOs face this challenge at 43% and Chinese CEOs at 24%. Global CEO survey. It reveals that two-thirds of UK CEOs mention that recruiting people with digital skills is difficult, compared with only 43% of CEOs in the US and just 24% in China. CEOs say that STEM skills are also harder to recruit in the UK than anywhere else. Behind these harrowing statistics, and my personal lived experience, there are wider societal problems at play, that we need to consider. A study by the Organization for Economic Co-operation and Development (OECD)[35] found that girls still lack the confidence to pursue high-paid careers, in science and technology. Despite their school results being as good as - or better than - those achieved by boys.

This persistent gender imbalance gap between men and women studying and working in Tech, isn't just wrong in societal terms. But unfair, when you consider women's skills and participation in the workforce. But think about the impact technology is having on our personal and working lives? Presently, technology is shaping the way of our way of living, with products and services that are being developed. Determined by the perspectives of only half of the population and not designed, with the needs of everyone in mind. Women make up half of consumers and technology companies need to reflect this in their workforce designing those products.

Technology Regulation

Black women experience barriers, when accessing STEM. Yet, political decisions, policies, and social dynamics can influence opportunities in STEM. I have seen, over the last three decades, how this has played out and who have been the winners and losers.

Good news though… Tech/Educational institutions, and Government research agencies, can design policies that create opportunities for Black women to enter, and advance in STEM careers. I, myself, have experienced the importance of access to quality education, and how this is fundamental to factors, in pursuing a career in STEM. I remember in my teaching career, whenever there was a new government introduced, they would inject funding into STEM opportunities to get more girls into this industry. The government has funded the #BeMedigitalinclusion program to encourage under-represented groups, to pursue STEM careers. This political support has been crucial to the programme's global success, and the enormous interest from Black women, getting involved. Policies can also influence change within the workplace, which relates to diversity, equity, and inclusion. For example, legislation such as anti-discrimination can shape the work environment for Black women in Tech. This will help address issues like pay disparities and workplace discrimination. Also, political decisions, related to, the regulation of emerging technologies, can have a significant impact on individuals. This was a major concern for me, when I advised the UN pulse on the Ethical use of AI, regarding issues like data privacy. When I spoke at *'The Future of Policing and Gang Crime Prevention 2021'* at the

Institute of Government and Public Policy. I mentioned the dangers of facial recognition use on our Black youths. Now, I am concerned about Internet access, and how this can, disproportionately, affect Black women in so many ways. For instance, the decision around digital redlining, relates to the mobilization and position of broadband installation. As this will involve excluding certain communities from high-speed Internet access. The impact will affect Black women, having limited access to online education, remote working, and tech entrepreneur opportunities. The effects of the cost-of-living crises and businesses not being able to attract and secure the services of staff. According to recent Digital research[36], they concluded that more than four, in five (81%) UK Managing Directors say, a lack of digital skills negatively affects their company.

Yet, we see that narrowing the gap, has become more of a challenge. On account of, ongoing challenges that Black people face, while looking to improve their digital skills. You can see that this is terrible news for all: Employees, businesses, and the UK economy–research has revealed that a shortage of digital skills costs the UK economy £12.8m. Furthermore, this will also create greater inequality, as lower-income individuals find their career and salary prospects, hampered.

We are seeing more products and services digitalized, and the growth prospects are becoming dependent on a sufficiently trained, tech-competent workforce. When we look at barriers to digital skills. We see exclusion from lower-income groups, from digital opportunities, because of unequal access to the required technologies. For example, access to the web allows you to work from home, search and apply for jobs, and learn vital ICT skills. Such as drafting and sending emails or creating Excel spreadsheets (the digital skills gap includes basic and advanced tech skills, too). Yet, in one study, the Office for National Statistics found that only 51% of households earning between £6,000-10,000 had home internet access. Compared with 99% of households with an income of over £40K. With millions struggling to keep up with escalating bills, this divide will probably worsen, as it forces more people to make financial concessions. Unfortunately, this is happening now!

Similarly, a lack of access to digital devices prevents self-learning. Our #BeMedigitalinclusion program has given 40 schools across London, devices to ensure that the #BeMedigitalinclusion women and girls can access our programs. In 2020, an Ofcom survey found that, nearly 1 in 10 households containing children, did not have home access to a laptop, desktop PC, or tablet. Therefore, learning becomes a challenge without a suitable notebook or computer, and especially because many coding courses, now require coursework, that are only available online.

Social mobility becomes increasingly difficult, if the tech or funds for training courses are unavailable. Indeed, research by Virgin Media and O2 found that 31% of UK workers believe, it passed them over for a promotion or pay rise, because they lacked adequate digital skills. Meaning, individuals hoping to find a higher-paying salary to support themselves during the cost-of-living crisis, cannot do so[37].

This picture, clearly shows that there is a digital skills gap within the Black community and lack of opportunities in accessing the jobs, compared to other communities.

This inequality is also the case for all women in the Tech industry. When we look at a new analysis from the British Computing Society (BCS). The Chartered Institute for Information Technology - a part of BCS - even though more women than ever, are working in IT roles across the UK (326,000) and make up a record 20% of the specialist IT workforce. Many of these women are in lower end and paid less than their male counterparts' jobs.

BAME Women in Tech

For BAME women in Tech, it is shocking! In 2019, an average of 9% of BAME IT specialists were at the Director level. 32% of BAME IT specialists were managers or team leaders, compared to 43% of white IT professionals. The average female representation of the FTSE 100 board is 33% and the real, enormous concern is the percentage of Black women in Tech. Over the past year, has seen a small increase of them working in IT positions - from 0.3% in 2019 to 0.7% in 2020. According to the BCS study, based on Office for National Statistics (ONS) June 2021 employment data. Black women are still acutely under-represented in IT and, by comparison, across other occupations where their level of representation is 2.5 times higher.

For Black girls, this crisis includes, difficulty accessing quality learning opportunities in Science, Technology, Engineering and Mathematics (STEM)–subjects, commonly ascribed to and dominated by boys and men, and lower levels of achievement in digital skills. Education systems have allowed gender divides to be perpetuated, and to disproportionally, affect most Black girls. While girls tend to outperform boys, in reading skills in most other areas. They also continue to be under-represented, amongst top performers in STEM subjects, and women continue to be underrepresented in the STEM workforce as evidenced, in previously shown data.

However, achievement in STEM subjects goes beyond digital access. It is about the skills that STEM learning cultivates, which can be applied throughout life, e.g. lateral thinking, problem-solving and innovating. In an age, shaped by technological advances. Having the know-how to operate, use and create technology and science-based solutions, will be critical in the advancement of young people. Equally, crucial for girls' and women in health, education, voice, and empowerment.

Education interventions, by government United Nations agencies, Private Sector, Non-Government Organization and Civil Society have worked somewhat in improving girls' access to education. Yet, there is not enough evidence to suggest that consistent quality education in safe, gender-responsive environments has been provided across the board. This affects Black girls' opportunities to learn to reach their fullest potential and transition into the workplace. The shortage of this type of learning wastes the educational potential to support, in transforming, the unequal gender expectations and harmful gender norms. If the purpose of primary and secondary schooling and vocational training, is to provide unbiased opportunities for Black girls, then it has failed! Having business as usual will NOT lead to an equality of opportunity and empowerment for every girl.

It is important to explain the journey of Black women and what they have experienced over the last five decades. Based on my twenty-plus years of experience in the teaching profession. Although, at times, understanding the historical context is being ignored, in relation to why Black women are constantly at the bottom. This helps to show how significant the #BeMeDigitalinclusion program is, and what it means, in ensuring our young girls do not experience what has gone before.

STEM and its Impact on Black Women and Society

The inaccessibility of education, that allows for greater representation in STEM, is far wider than just the absence of Black girls in technology. There's a broader societal impact.

Black Women in Social Housing

The inequalities, faced by Black women, prior to Covid-19, will greatly affect them in the post-Covid era and '*new normal*'. If ignored, the lack of opportunity will be a factor in issues such as, mental ill-health. In the current state, 90% of Black women who live in social housing, do not own their own homes and are more likely to be a single parent[38]. Therefore, depending on where they live, they may not have access to the internet/ICT, which will hinder activity online, further, widening their digital skills gap.

Single Parenting and Health

We know that access to health care is crucial for overall wellbeing and career success. Black women who experience healthcare disparities are affected by political decisions on healthcare access. So, when we look at Black pregnant women, they are more likely to experience complications. If a Black woman is in a relationship, they are ten times more likely to experience domestic violence, with no support system in place and neglected by the state. Since, what is now available caters for the needs of white women being a single mother and lacking parental support (from a partner). This can have a detrimental impact on her and the family, causing severe stress, which sometimes leads to illness. Black women still faced problems when they were pregnant and attended the hospital. Considering, they are more likely to have complications, ending up either dying or their child being too ill. These kinds of factors also create a situation where it is difficult to really support a child in choosing the right path to get into STEM subjects, as the focus is on improving their lives for the better.

Impact of Covid-19 on Families

Many Black women have failed relationships with their families, which further emphasizes, a lack of support mechanisms to help them, in their daily life. This is a genuine concern within the community, because the long-term impact is so severe. For example, being unable to have a favourable job to pay for things needed within the home, leads to resentment.

More and more families are experiencing poverty and the impact of Covid-19. Parents, have, either been made redundant or furloughed, or left to homeschool their children, without, the actual expertise. This is a big problem, because their children are not accessing quality education or being exposed to STEM opportunities. Also, most of these families cannot sign up to digital schooling, given that, they do not have the correct digital devices. Or are not linked to the internet, since they cannot afford it.

Black Women in Employment

In the workplace, Black women are treated unfairly, earning less than their counterparts - white men and women. They are often sidelined and restricted in their job/career progression, 'invisible', until something goes wrong. Most times, it makes them feel humiliated and yet, still expected to do the same, or more than others. A recent UN report on women shows that by 2021, 485m women and girls, will be pushed into extreme poverty.

Politics and STEM

This is the intersection of how political decisions have affected Black women - this includes the decision around algorithm policies, too. As a tech disruptor, I love the prospect that Tech affords. I want to actually draw from the role of Politics, STEM and girls, using a real-life example, on how it impacts Black women. I want you to think about how the use of AI Tech can promote economic growth, increase productivity at a lower cost, create jobs, and more? All this looks promising, and you can clearly see an economic boost. Consequently, in most organizations, we are seeing opportunities in education | housing | employment and more. But as they deem this AI tech, a smart economic investment for the future, we need to pause. Whose future and whose wallets are we talking about? It is necessary, that I take you on a journey of a Black woman, living under this guise.

Paulette Watson

Case Study

Sarah has three children, and living in London's most deprive borough. She had left school with no qualifications and experienced a tough childhood. Her mother was a victim of Domestic Violence (DV), having to flee, and this resulted in Sarah and her siblings going into care and being separated. Sarah suffered from further abuse within the care system, and this had an adverse effect on her mental health. She was also gang raped twice and ended up getting pregnant. Now, with two children, living in temporary accommodation and receiving welfare benefits. Sarah has now gained employment and sends her children to school. She wants to move to a better place and start a fresh. However, this is proving a real challenge, because of her historical background and being unable to move forward. Unfortunately, this is the case for a lot of Black women, in this situation in London.

A snapshot analysis of government figures by London

Councils. Revealed that 42,000 people living in temporary accommodation in the English capital identified as female, compared to 21,700 adult males.[39] Securing housing is a real challenge, and this has been the case over the last 30 years. My concern now, is how AI tools will perpetuate housing discrimination. For example, AI systems, used to evaluate potential tenants, relies on core records and other datasets that have their own, built-in biases. To reflect systemic racism, sexism, and ableism - which are all, full of errors. They deny Black women housing, despite being able to pay rent, because the tenant screening algorithms, deem them ineligible or unworthy.

You can see these algorithms use data, such as eviction and criminal histories. That clearly reflect, long-standing racial disparities in housing and the criminal legal system, which are discriminatory, towards Black women.

We know that Black women, wanting to purchase homes or re-finance, have been charged an arm and a leg, by these AI tools, used by lenders. Another issue I have, in which, I just recently withdrew my application from. It is, companies using AI driven tools, to interview and screen jobseekers, which pose enormous risks for Black women, and particularly those with disabilities, and others in protected groups. If we are not careful, AI may continue to exclude us and add to our discriminatory experiences.

Governments, need to take concrete steps, to bring our civil rights and equity to the forefront, in A.I technologies policies. In addition to, conscientiously, addressing the systemic harms of these technologies.

Chapter 3–Race, Gender & Technology[40]

The #BeMedigitalincluison Program

Why is the #BeMedigitalincluison program important? How will AI impact on getting black girls in STEM | AI related careers?

Artificial Intelligence (A.I.) Ethics.

Artificial Intelligence (A.I.) Ethics is a system of moral principles and techniques intended to inform the development and responsible use of artificial intelligence technology. The Three Laws of Robotics (often shortened to The Three Laws (or known as Asimov's Laws) are rules devised by Isaac Asimov. These regulations introduced were in his 1942 short story, "Runaround" (included in the 1950 collection "I, Robot"). The Three Laws, quoted from the "Handbook of Robotics, 56th Edition, 2058 A.D.", Asimov, Isaac (1950). "Runaround. "I, Robot" (The Isaac Asimov Collection, ed.). "Introduction." The Rest of the Robots. Doubleday.[41]

- First Law: A robot may not injure a human being or, through inaction, allow a human being to come to harm.

- Second Law: A robot must obey the orders given by human beings, except where such orders would conflict with the First Law.

- Third Law: A robot must protect its existence, if, such protection does not conflict with the First or Second Law.

In Asimov's Code of Ethics, the first law forbids robots from actively harming humans or allowing harm to humans by refusing to act. In essence, the three rules are essential in spearheading the #BeMedigitalinclusion project in raising the aspiration of a million Black women and girls into Science, Technology, Engineering and Maths, and related careers. Isaac Asimov (1964)[42]. Refers to the simulation of human intelligence in machines, programmed to think like humans and mimic our actions. This term exhibits traits associated with a human mind, such as learning and problem-solving.

When you think about it, AI is a computational problem-solving mechanism. The data is used to teach the machine how to make specific decisions and test its performance against an answer key. Then the training wheels are removed, and there you have it; the computer can complete the decision process independently, on new data. In the same vein, the computer can learn and select certain demographics and discriminatory outcomes. My concern here is when the data used to train these computers is collected without consent or at risk of personal privacy[43]. For me, this process contributes to a system of algorithmic bias, in which we have now seen that, some algorithms result in replicating and even amplifying human biases and those, affecting protected groups.[44]

According to Gartner, a research company. They predict that 85 percent of AI projects will deliver incorrect outcomes because of algorithmic bias.[45] I know that marginalized groups, such as women and Black people, will be adversely affected by the erroneous algorithms.

Here, I want to share some examples of how AI discriminates Black women in Health, Education, Recruitment and Policing. AI driven healthcare algorithms have shown racial bias. Especially, when used for predicting patient risk levels. This has resulted in systematically under diagnosing or undertreatment in Black women. This bias, can lead to delayed or inadequate medical intervention, contributing to a disparity in health outcomes. We should also examine how AI, considerably relies on the data set, they are trained on.

Black Girls and Artificial Intelligence

Historically, Black women have been subjected to abuse, using the A.I. tool. The Gender Shades Project, is a research initiative, led by Dr Joy Buolamwini. She has exposed, glaring biases in facial analysis technology, employed by major tech companies. Dr. Joy's investigation started when her photo went undetected by specific systems, and others labelled her as male. It resulted in a comprehensive analysis of 1,270 unique faces. Unearthing significant gender and skin type biases in AI-based gender classification. The results from this study, revealed alarming statistics.

The worst-case scenario demonstrated that these systems failed to correctly classify, darker-skinned females, more than one, in three times, despite a 50% chance of accuracy. Conversely, the best-performing classifier illustrated a flawless 0% error rate in classifying lighter-skinned males. It is clear, that this research, starkly underscores the deep-rooted biases in commercial AI systems. Especially in terms of gender and skin type. Calling for urgent attention and rectification within the tech industry.

The study also exposed skin type and gender bias in commercial A.I. products, from IBM, Microsoft, Amazon, and more, galvanizing research and public attention, to issues of algorithmic bias. The study found that Amazon's system–*Recognition*, had much more difficulty, telling the gender of females with darker-skinned faces in photos, than similar services, from IBM and Microsoft. Sadly, instead of offering a way to address fairer performance results. Amazon's Web Service executives, in multiple blog posts, attempted to discredit the study by co-authors, Joy Buolamwini and Deb Raji. Still, thankfully, this was rebuked by over 70 respected A.I. researchers, who defended the findings and called on Amazon to stop selling the technology to the police. A position, the company started using last year, after the death of George Floyd.

This treatment is more profound than what has happened, and interestingly, the same historical tactics, used against Black women for centuries, continues today. Here, I want to share some examples of how AI discriminates Black women in health, education, recruitment and policing.

AI driven healthcare algorithms have shown, racial bias, especially when used for predicting patient risk levels. This has resulted in, systematically, under diagnosing or undertreatment in Black women. This bias can lead to delayed or inadequate medical intervention, contributing to disparity in health outcomes. We should also consider how AI relies heavily on the data set it is trained on.

You and I know that, the medical research dataset lacks diversity and predominately represents non-white populations. The sad thing is, is that the AI systems will not accurately account for the unique health factors and risk faced by Black women. Leading to misdiagnosed and ineffective treatment recommendations. As an educator, with my understanding of analysing data in education. I know they could use AI systems for personalized learning and grading. The issue I have with this, is that, if these systems are trained on data that reflects historical educational biases. For instance, Black Afro Caribbean girls underachieving in their A-C GCSE results. The ramifications of this, may perpetuate those biases further. This could justify offering less challenging coursework and provide lower grades to Black women students, limiting their educational opportunities. Another example that has affected me personally, is AI-driven, recruitment tools. These can inadvertently discriminate against Black women. Biased algorithms could potentially favour candidates with names and background perceived as more functional, thus overlooking highly qualified perspectives and skills in the workplace. Can you see a trend here? Black women's experiences are being replicated in every sphere of life. We have become so used to this, that we are living in a state, where we are so removed from everyday life. We must be in the present! I say this because of the situation concerning our children.

Still today, our young Black girls are being abused at the hands of the police force. Recently, a London Metropolitan Service police officer callously hit a vulnerable Black girl over '30 times' with a baton and was dismissed from the police service. Many police officers cause pain whether to a male, female, child, or adult. There's no distinction, just rage, and a mission to kill and destroy. The same tactics seen and used on George Floyd's murder and, quite honestly, no different from how Black women experience unfair treatment in the tech industry. The same white men are the ones who are creating the algorithmic codes, The 'Abuse and Misogynoir Playbook' published by a trio of MIT researchers, Moya Bailey, coined the term "misogynoir," in 2010. As a portmanteau of "misogyny" and "noir." Playbook co-authors Katlyn Turner, Danielle Wood, and Catherine D'Ignazio, say these tactics are also used to disparage former Ethical A.I. team co-lead Timnit Gebru. After Google fired her in late 2020, because of stress. Something, that needs to be recognized by engineers and data scientists.

Timnit Gebru[46] is a prominent artificial-intelligence computer scientist. Who helped pioneer research, into facial recognition software's biases, against people of colour. Then got fired from Google, after forwarding a scathing email - She felt, the company's treatment of minority employees, were being *"constantly dehumanized."* Reading Timnit's experience with Google, is very distressing. Especially, since, Google previously fired employees, who advocated for increased diversity or critiqued the company's ethics.

My concerns are with the everyday use of the internet. How discrimination is embedded in computer code and, to a greater degree, in artificial intelligence technologies, that we rely on. By choice or not, our human rights are being impinged on every single day, and this is becoming a global phenomenon. So far, we understand the long-term impact of these decision-making tools on both masking and deepening social inequalities. The #BeMedigitalinclusion program is the catalyst for making this impact visible for all to see. *How do we navigate the effects of automated decision-making through an algorithmic tool in our society?* The real challenge here, is that many Black women dislike mathematics. Yet, the challenge of understanding algorithmic oppression, is that those mathematical formulations, which drive automated decisions; - human beings create it! When we consider the new and emerging technologies, Big Data, IoT, A.I., Mixed Reality, Quantum computing, Genomics, and more. We think they are there to create opportunities for our girls, but they are not. The same people who create these codes, use these data structures and make the rules. These, hold differing views, values, and beliefs that openly promote racism, sexism, and discrimination at all levels. Safiya Umoja, Noble Algorithms of oppression, as described above.

But we also need to stop and think about the representation these big corporations, namely, Google, have shown Black women. In 2015, a U.S. News and

World Report reported a "glitch" in Google's algorithms, that led to several problems through auto-tagging and facial recognition software. Intended to help people search for images more successfully. These tools had major issues; firstly, Google's photo application had automatically tagged African Americans as "apes" and "animals." Equally, Google Maps searches on the word "N*gger" led to a map of the White House during Obama's presidency. This story went viral when social media personality DeRay McKesson tweeted it. We need to understand what type of person/people would tag people as animals. When working with computers, you have low-level languages (machine code) and high-level languages (python). It takes *'someone'* to write the algorithms, since computers only put out what they receive.

Sadly, these continued data aberrations and practices have been highlighted with reports of Photoshopped monkey face images, on the appearance of the First Lady Michelle Obama, that were circulating through the Google images search in 2009. Again, in 2015, digital traces of the Google autosuggestions linked Michelle Obama with apes. However, Google made clear that, it is not responsible for its algorithm, but it was willing to resolve these issues. In the Washington Post article about "N*gger House": "…some inappropriate results are surfing up in Google Maps that should not be, and we apologize for any offence this may have caused."

So, there you have it! These human and computer codes are not without consequences and show how racism and sexism are part of the architecture. The language of technology, and the #BeMeDigitalinclusion project, will need to address these inherent issues within these A.I. digital tools. A.I. systems, from leading companies, that have failed to correctly classify the faces of Oprah Winfrey, Michelle Obama, and Serena Williams. So, when technology denigrates even these iconic women, we know, it is time to re-examine the structure of these systems and who they serve.

If our #BeMeDigitalinclusion, girls are silenced and feel dehumanized. How are they supposed to operate and give culturally, and be innovative? The tech industry needs to be diversified to create better and safer products, that includes everyone, not just one social group. Yet, a 2020 report from McKinsey showed that companies that employ people from diverse communities, perform better, recruit better talent, have more engaged employees. Also, being able to enlist workers, better than companies that do not focus on diversity and inclusion. However, women remain widely underrepresented in I.T. roles. Statistics from the following nine facets of I.T. work, ranging from higher education to the workplace surroundings. Paint a clear picture of the challenges women face, in finding an equal footing, in a career in I.T.

According to a new analysis, from the British Computer Society (BSC), The Chartered Institute for I.T. More women than ever are working in I.T. roles across the U.K. (326,000 in total) and they make up a record 20% share of the specialist I.T. workforce. The volume of women in specialist computing roles, increased to its highest ever level this summer (2020). Rising to 20% from 17% at the same point in 2019, the professional body for I.T. found.

According to a BCS study, based on Office for National Statistics (ONS) employment data. There has been a slight increase in Black women working in I.T. positions, from 0.3% in 2009 to 0.7% in 2020. Yet, Black women are still crushingly, under-represented in I.T. and, by comparison, their level of representation is 2.5 times higher across other occupations. As a whole, 31,000 Black people were working in I.T. positions across the U.K. in the second quarter of the year (2020) - 1.9% of the total I.T. specialist workforce.

Black women face the following discriminations in these areas:

- Employment,
- Retention,
- Workplace culture issues,
- Lack of representation: pay gaps and leadership positions,
- Covid-19 pandemic's impact on Black women in tech are more likely to lose their jobs than men and

are more likely to feel significant childcare burdens,

- Mental health.

As you can see, there's a lot of work to be done to diversify the tech industry. This should not be a tick-box process but be at the top of the agenda, to close the diversity gap and create a professional, highly skilled, and ethical I.T workspace culture.

Predictive Software Technology

Another tool that causes concern is predictive software technology. Predictive analytics software, mines, and analyses historical data patterns, predict future outcomes by extracting information from data sets, to determine patterns and trends. Machines can discriminate in harmful ways. After watching coding bias on Netflix, I was just overwhelmed with the findings and Joy Buolamwini's personal experience, increases my fear of what Black girls could encounter, if things are not corrected now. Joy discovered that, some facial analysis software, could not detect her dark-skinned face. Not until she placed a white mask over it. The trained images of predominantly light-skinned men have demonstrated, in her experience, the *'coded gaze'*. The bias in artificial intelligence could lead to discriminatory or exclusionary practices. Too often, Black women must change, how we are to fit within the status quo. In this case, it is better represented by a '*white mask*', than our own Black faces. The impact of digital exclusion will continue. If we do not address, the inherent bias that plagues our Black women, through the lenses of the intersectionality of humanity and understand the levels of racism experienced. How much, will Black girls, have to change themselves, to function with technological systems, that increasingly govern our lives?

Machines are not neutral, even though it may appear to be the case. Joy's further research, uncovered a significant gender and racial bias in A.I. systems, sold by tech giants like IBM, Microsoft, and Amazon. To which, they were given the task of guessing the gender of a face. All companies performed substantially better on male faces than female faces. The companies, she evaluated had an error rate of marginally, 1% for lighter-skinned men, but for darker-skinned women, the errors soared to 35%.

As mentioned earlier, A.I. systems from leading companies, have failed to correctly classify the faces of Oprah Winfrey, Michelle Obama, and Serena Williams. What will our Black girl's fate be, if this is happening with these iconic women now? They need to be represented in the design, development, deployment, and governance of A.I. creating and building these systems, so they can dispel the unrealized and unbiased algorithms.

Oppressive Algorithms

Algorithms of Oppression are text-based on over six years of academic research on Google search algorithms. The book addresses the relationship between search engines and discriminatory biases.

Safiya Umoja Noble's work has been of great interest, especially when designing the #BeMeDigitalinclusion project. Nearly a decade ago, she Googled 'Black Girls' and the search results, were mostly pornographic. She went on to explore, how algorithms can perpetuate discrimination and inequality. Thankfully, Google could fix that search engine issue. But we are nowhere near solving this problem. The research found Google's advertising platform linked the search phrase, to adult content ads. Alarmingly, oppressing Black girls without them even knowing.

"Algorithms of oppression are everywhere," Sariya said. "I'm talking about computational software embedded in large-scale platforms – or even household brands – used to disenfranchise, marginalize, and misrepresent." That Google's search engine is built, to assume those looking for information about Black girls, were interested in pornography "reinforced misrepresentations," Noble said.

When creating a #BeMedigitalinclusion strategy and searching platforms, such as Instagram GIFs on STEM and Black girls, nothing came up in the search. It left a sense of cynicism, as the constant stereotypes do not represent Black girls. Exacerbated, by filters which are dull, and the content is not engaging enough to entice

Black girls. It is hard to believe that, in 2021, there is no representation of Black girls in STEM. To realize parity, companies must ensure access for Black girls to build products and create career opportunities.

Although, Google claim, they have an extensive staffed team, working on scalable solutions. However, after searching Black Girls (30th June 2021), they are still, not committed to making diversity, equity, or inclusion part of their everyday mantra. There is concern about these search engines and the algorithms used in these 'cloud' technologies, from predictive policing software[47,48] facial recognition tools, to social media platforms; accelerate disinformation.

These technologies, sanction minorities for unfair treatment and provide little recourse to redress. Safiya states, *'these technologies'* are specifically deployed, towards vulnerable people frequently communities of colour, poor people, who are the least empowered to resist."

Greater diversity in the technology industry will help. As the harm towards vulnerable groups cannot be erased or forgotten, the lessons learned when moving forward, especially in our case. As we roll out the #BeMedigitalinclusion project, to raise the aspiration, of one million Black girls in Science, Technology, Engineering, Maths, and related careers; is to ensure there is parity in the tech industry. Thus, it is essential to rectify the flaws in this system and ensure that Black girls design these algorithms. As a result of, helping to eliminate unrealized biases in their communities, countries, and around the world.

Chapter 4–STEM, the Economy & Economics in the U.K. & the World

STEM's Role in the Economy

Introduction

"There must be a stream of new scientific knowledge to turn the wheels of private and public enterprise. There must be plenty of men and women trained in science and technology, for upon them depend on both the creation of new knowledge and its application to practical purposes." Vannevar Bush, 1951.[49]

Innovation - primarily through invention, development, and a profusion of new technologies - is the fundamental source of economic progress. The inventive activity is strongly associated with economic growth in urban, rurally and nationally. Technological innovation requires the expertise of specialists with knowledge. In the fields of science, technology, engineering, and mathematics, as discussed throughout this book and known as STEM.[50]

As of 2011, 26m U.S. jobs, 20% of all jobs, required knowledge in any STEM field. Since the Industrial

Revolution, these jobs have doubled from less than 10% in 1850 to 20% in 2010. Pause for a moment and imagine the impact of STEM on the economy. By examining the companies and products that have revolutionized our lives, e.g., Google, Apple, Meta, Amazon, and Microsoft (GAMAM). The list is endless and within each company STEM powers all of them, and these are essential skills to have. Especially when building and maintaining success within the economy of any country.

Integral to any nation's development, every ounce of human life relies on scientists' and engineers' discoveries and creativity. Consider, a medical scientist who develops treatments for diseases and civil engineers, who design and build a nation's infrastructure. STEM is significant now, and will continue to be, in years to *come*. Children and Young People (CYP) need to be equipped with science, technology, and engineering maths to be more competitive, internationally. This will help to generate new creative and innovative ideas for the future. Preparing our #BeMedigitalinclusion of young women and girls, with the essential skills, that will advance our nation. Encouraging them to do everything, from building roads and bridges to conducting life-saving medical research.

Breaking down, STEM and its broader role:

- *STEM drives productivity* and, since 1980, aggregate productivity in Research & Development (R&D) and STEM-heavy. Industries have increased far faster than in the rest of the economy. Thus, supporting sectors that drive productivity growth is essential during slowed growth.

- *STEM generates high-earning potential.* STEM workers earn, on average (in the UK), £14,000 yearly, more than non-STEM workers at, practically, every education level.

- *STEM creates new jobs.* The STEM workforce will grow by at least 75m workers between 2022-2026 according to the World Economic Forum (WEF) report: *The Future of Jobs 2018*[51]. U.S. Senator Martin Heinrich in his paper, *Ten Ways STEM Strengthens the Economy*, highlights this too[52].

- *STEM offers middle-skills pathways.* In 2018, 35% of all STEM job openings did not require a bachelor's degree. Together, with most jobs needing at least some post-secondary education. Such as, an associate degree, industry-recognised credential, or similar certificate.[53]

- *STEM increases women's earnings.* Women in STEM earn 33% more than women in non-STEM jobs, but the under-representation of women in these jobs, is shocking!

- *STEM closes racial and ethnic wage gaps.* Racial and ethnic wage gaps are more significant in STEM than in non-STEM occupations. We must increase minority participation in STEM fields because it is essential to boost earnings among workers of colour and narrowing wage gaps.

- *STEM connects rural workers to jobs requiring STEM skills and knowledge.* Traditional "non-STEM" jobs now require a STEM background. Including health, manufacturing, and agriculture employment in rural communities.

- *STEM addresses income inequality.* Metropolitan areas, with a higher concentration of middle-skill STEM workers, perform better on various economic indicators, including lower-income inequality levels.

- *STEM spurs innovation through 'Research & Development'.* Increasing R&D investment by two to four times the current level would produce the most effective economic growth rate.[54]

- *STEM supports high-growth industries like computer science.* Computer-based occupations will increase by 12.5% in 2024, resulting in nearly half a million new jobs (in the United States).[55]

We should not underestimate the importance of STEM today, since its role will be steadily significant within a short time. We have seen and experienced that today's technology alters people's lives faster. Therefore, it is vital for countries seeking to reduce their poverty levels. To adopt new scientific research and technology and, in doing so, improve their economy, health care system, and infrastructure. For developing countries, this is intrinsically important.

How Important is STEM Concerning the Broader Economy

Overall, four sectors - Health, Education, Housing, and Employment–I will explain how and why STEM is essential to each. Since, digital technology has been booming, and this has been the case, for the last ten years.

Health

mHealth is a mobile application for health and well-being and connected wearable devices. This emerging market is still small and fragmented. However, there is an increase in use of mHealth by consumers, who are being decisive about their wellness. This technology supports higher-impact clinical decision-making and improves clinician and patient interaction.

This app will be the fastest-growing segment in digital health, with 35% in the UK and 49% worldwide[56]. Right now, the health apps market is in two groups:

1. One group handles low confidentiality data. (Personal wellness and activity data), usually a

consumer-driven purchase, has attracted multiple companies into the space, **e.g. Google and Apple products**.

2. The second group manages medium to high confidentiality data (health data and personal medical records) that clinicians and patients use. Hospital systems reporting mHealth solutions, in the second group. Offers the potential to improve healthcare outcomes. But this, presents challenges until further access to data, is enhanced.[57]

More importantly, for our #BeMedigitalinclusion of young females. Inequality in the health sector, especially amongst the Black community, has been provoked further, since Covid-19. Therefore, equipping our young females digitally, as app developers, will enable them to understand the correct data structures to use, create and design the algorithms. This will return, invaluable information about grassroots health problems experienced, within their community. They will create a platform, where they own and protect their data from any eyes, trying to steal their information. They will hold and be the owner of their data and decide who they want to communicate it with. Including how they wish to distribute the relevant information to key stakeholders. For instance, the authorities, to help address their local community needs. Using their high levels of digital literacy and adoption will help create and solve problems by adding value to mHealth app companies around London, the U.K. and worldwide.

Health analytics software solutions, and analytical capabilities, can help identify what is happening. In its infancy, this tech is still a fast-growing part of the digital health sector, up 24% in 2018. If the U.K. is clever, it can be the world's leader in this sector; however, the existing barriers make it a real challenge for our #BeMedigitalinclusion of young women and girls. For instance, lack of training opportunities, retention issues, microaggression in the work environment, cultural issues, pay gaps. Inclusive of unfair treatment of ethnic minority staff, needs when developing relevant skills and capabilities. This can assist in *'levelling the playing field'*.[58,59]

We must ensure that, young women and girls in #BeMedigitalinclusion have access to these opportunities in the health analytics industry. There are challenges around data access, that can help to maximize an industry's growth. Along with, the resources that must develop the #BeMedigitalinclusion programme, to ensure that the UK's infrastructure is accessible and uses data to build the sector and address the inequalities.

Digitized health systems: digital health, information, storage, and exchange of patient and medical records, are in primary care and hospital information systems, which are essential for collecting data for health analytics. These sectors face many similar drivers and challenges. However, they have different maturity levels, growth rates, and market penetration. Digital health is the largest, yet slowest growing, sector in the U.K. Including Electronic Health Records (EHR) and e-prescribing, with a total current market size of £1.3bn.[60]

Focus On the Demand for Stem Jobs & Skills in Britain[61]

Where technological advancements are being made. Acute hospitals have lagged and are at the forefront of recent government initiatives. The UK is a frontrunner, in using primary care electronic health records, because of early government initiatives, to support system uptake. Incentivizing the use of EHR platforms, and investing in interoperability, will help the market reach its potential. The systems will move healthcare data securely across organizations. Store highly confidential data, safely link data sets together, and deliver consistent analytical methodologies that support clinical decision-making. These actions are necessary to help improve the quality and efficiency of health care, while maintaining patient confidentiality.

The problems include:

- A lack of commercialization skills.

- Shortages of I.T. and analytical capabilities.

- Difficulties in funding.

- Challenges with accessing local revenue stream in the National Health Service (NHS).

The Government's role is crucial in providing the infrastructure, such as regulatory frameworks and information governance, to support the sector's growth. In addition, the Government needs to consider investing in the #BeMedigitalinclusion project, to ensure that they leave no one behind.

Education

The overlap between education and innovation affects productivity by focusing on education in STEM. These fields produce workers who can meet the growing science - and technology-based innovation, at the core of modern economic growth. Conceptualizing labour quality and technology and innovation in STEM education growth, can be complex. It is assumed, in most national jurisdictions, that the quantity and quality of STEM competencies, affect economic performance. Yet, Marginson et al. (2013) cited that educational quality, when measured by cognitive skills. Primarily, in science and mathematics, is an accurate predictor of a more significant influence on economic outcomes, than the general quality of education. In their analysis of STEM education in various countries. Marginson et al. Concluded widespread interest in building high-end STEM skills was linked to research, development, and industry innovation. The Department for Business, Energy, and Strategy's UK Innovate Strategy, wants to invest millions, giving people opportunities to be innovators in technology. For this reason, a key focus should be to improve the overall quality of the human capital supply. Growing the high-skill group, capable of research, innovation, and effective responses to technological transformation.

In terms of subject choices, over half (51%) of Black students who took A-levels in maths, biology, chemistry, and physics were girls. Boys still outnumbered girls across all ethnicities, with "white other" girls showing the lowest uptake (41%) of STEM Courses. When we consider the attainment levels in these subjects, Black females do exceptionally well in science, technology, engineering, and maths.[62] I found this key focus very ambitious. Especially when you consider the experiences of a Black female, through the lens of intersectionality, having to deal with their ethnicity, disability, sexuality, and gender.

Although there were a higher percentage of entries of Black females in STEM, they were more likely to pick the subjects at a lower rate than their peers. Of all the Black girls studying A-levels, only 12% took STEM; of all pupils in the country taking these subjects, 13% were Black, 13% White British, while Pakistani/Bangladeshi pupils made up 18%, and "other Asian" pupils 28%[63]. These equalities continue to persist for Black females when entering higher education. Something happens when they leave 6th form; they have the grades, but are discouraged, to pursue subjects that will positively affect their economic status, of being financially free. It is as if these young females experience another level of discrimination that still significantly impacts their mental health[64].

According to the Higher Education Statistics Agency (HESA), in 2018-2019, over half (57.1%) of students enrolled in higher education were women. In the said year, women were over half of all enrolled students and graduates at the undergraduate and postgraduate levels. Women were 58.5% of all enrolled students at the postgraduate level and 59.6% of graduates. In 2018–2019, across several subject areas of higher education, women were underrepresented, including:

- Computer Science 18.4%
- Engineering and Technology 19.1%
- Mathematical Sciences 37.2%
- Architecture, Building, and Planning 38.5%
- Physical Sciences 43.3%
- Business and Administrative Studies 49.3%

In their analysis of STEM education in various countries. Marginson et al. concluded that research, development, and industry innovation in high-end STEM skills go hand in hand. They assumed STEM education in most national jurisdictions affects the quantity and quality of STEM competencies, and therefore affects economic performance too.

Half (50%) of all STEM jobs is available to workers without a degree, and these jobs pay £50,000+ on average, a wage 10% higher than jobs with similar educational requirements. The UK's STEM skills shortage is well-documented, costing employers £1.5bn a year in additional training, recruitment, temporary staffing and a further £2bn a year in additional training, recruitment and temporary staffing and inflated salaries. So, from 2003 to 2017, STEM job growth exceeded non-STEM job growth (by 4.5% age points), and this trend is expected to continue for the foreseeable future. The low number of graduates entering STEM occupations is of concern for employers. Since this is vital to economic development and international competitiveness - warning that a lack of talent could put off foreign investment, and over half (56%) expect the shortage to worsen in the next decade.[65]

Yet, with the increase in STEM undergraduates, over the past few years. Two-fifths of employers cited a shortage of STEM graduates as a critical barrier to recruiting appropriate staff. Nine in ten (89%) STEM employers report that the recruitment process takes much longer than usual[66], forcing many to resort to expensive solutions. STEM Learning found that over three-quarters (76%) inflate salaries to attract appropriately skilled workers, while nearly half (48%) have to look abroad to fill positions adequately. Half of all STEM jobs are in manufacturing, health care, or construction industries. Jobs in installation, maintenance, and repair account for 12% of STEM jobs, one of the largest categories[67]. Other blue-collar or technical jobs in construction and production also frequently demand STEM knowledge. It seems as if they gear the blame towards these young females, being economically disadvantaged. Still, we must delve deeper–we need to consider the living conditions of these young females. Their family's mental health and well-being, cultural aspect, and perceptions on these matters. Also, *who do these young females look up to, and who are their role models? What personal lived experiences have they heard from other women who have worked in the U.K. corporate world, and how has this affected them? And what are they doing now?*

If the UK wants to lead economically, they need to consider these issues. Given that McKinsey first published the report, *'Why Diversity Matters'* (2015). The likelihood of diverse companies outperforming industry, peers, while profitability, has increased significantly and penalties are getting steeper, for those lacking diversity. However, with all these inequalities, and injustices happening amongst our #BeMedigitalinclusion. Young females, despite not having the correct access to the tech space. This will have a massive impact on the UK's economy and to address this issue, we must do more to combat it.

In the UK, over-concentration of Black households in the most deprived neighbourhoods, is linked to poor housing conditions and lower economic status. Some of (Marmot's social determinants), ensures negative effects on health. Culminating in, lower life expectancy and higher morbidity rates, amongst ethnic minorities.[68]

Michael Marmot's social determinants of health frameworks, emphasizes, how various social and economic factors, can influence health outcomes. But more importantly, to our overall well-being, when we look at how digital inequalities faced by Black women, and how several determinants contribute to disparities in access to, and use of, digital technologies,

We know that the socioeconomic status, is a critical social determinant of health, and it directly affects access to digital resources. For instance, Black women disproportionately represented in lower-income communities have limited financial resources and cannot afford high-speed internet connections, computers, or smartphones. Without access to these digital tools, they face significant barriers to engaging in online education. Including access to healthcare information and pursuing job opportunities that require digital skills. Discrimination and bias, lead to digital inequalities, and many Black women experience this in online spaces. Resulting in harassment and exclusion. As a result, these experiences deter them from engaging in digital communities, being involved in online education, or seeking health information online. Another determinant of digital access is geographic location; Black women living in rural or underserved areas may have limited access to broadband internet, making it difficult to engage in online activities effectively, exacerbating inequalities in education, employment, and housing.

I'm particularly interested in housing for Black women, as this contributes to our overall wellbeing. Once our house is in order, then things ' *start to flow* ' perfectly.

Housing: Smart Homes

A smart home, means your home has an intelligent home system that connects with your appliances to automate specific tasks and control remotely. You can use a smart home system to program your sprinklers, set and monitor your home security system and cameras, or control appliances like your refrigerator, air conditioning, and heating[69].

What Impact Will Smart Homes Have On #BeMedigitalinclusion women?

Smart home systems will help improve. #BeMedigitalinclusion female residents' quality of life, will be helped, by providing various services, that assist them daily. There are four types, associated with home services: healthcare, energy, convenience, and security.

Firstly, access to healthcare services will enable #BeMedigitalinclusion women and girl's users, to manage their daily health, via a monitoring infrastructure (e.g., a smart thermometer, health data management platform, and fall detection). It will detect environmental information and potentially affect the residents' health, such as air quality and pollution[70].

Secondly, smart homes will reduce the impact of the environmental and economic costs of housing by reducing energy consumption and maintenance costs. Energy management services, provide residents with information that can reduce energy consumption in the house. Or automatically optimize energy consumption, without human intervention[71].

Convenience services are a crucial support, for the lifestyle of residents to help increase comfort. For example, environmental control is the most theoretical and representative smart home function. Environmental control includes remotely controlling or automatically scheduling house components. Such as thermostats, ventilators, lighting equipment, kitchen appliances, and various household appliances. It enables easy management of residential environments, effectively reducing household labour and providing comfort for #BeMedigitalinclusion female residents.

Lastly, smart home safety services can assist residents in managing the security of their homes and preventing accidents. For example, security services detect movements in the house to identify potential intruders or warn of open doors and windows.

A smart home lets you have peace of mind, by interfacing with your smartphone or tablet. Connecting the device and appliance in your home, so they can communicate with each other and with you - how cool is that? We can put any device in your home that uses electricity on your home network and at your command.[72] You have a choice to speak that command by voice, remote control, tablet, or smartphone; the home reacts - you are in control. Most applications relate to lighting, home security, theatre, and entertainment, and thermostat regulation. When considering a smart home, you could think of George Jetson and his futuristic abode.[73] Smart homes and home automation are becoming more common, and we can experience this tech-savvy lifestyle.

Smart homes are good, but there are some disadvantages to them too, such as smart home devices are expensive to buy:

- The cost[74]; the doorbell costs £150;
- A smart thermostat can cost over £250 compared to a programmable thermostat (which offers very similar improvements to your heating bills) which can be less than £100, including installation[75];
- A smart spotlight bulb could cost over £50 - so think about it, for each room, you could spend over £400 to kit it out.

So, as you can see, the high cost of many smart devices is a barrier to our #BeMedigitalinclusion females from buying loads of smart home products. Another concern is to do with the environment. As within some electrical components, rare earth metals are essential materials for many smart home devices; think about those that use batteries and lots of plastic? The process of making and delivering smart gadgets, made from mining raw materials, has a negative impact on our environment. I want you to consider the process of all this affecting our ecology. We must consider the impact of internet traffic too.

As much as 70% of internet traffic goes through a low-energy zone in Washington, DC, with only 3% of that energy being from renewable sources (with Greenpeace calculating that the rest–97%–comes from coal, gas, and nuclear power)[76]. Ultimately, Raghavan and Ma[77] estimated that the Internet uses 84 to 143 gigawatts of electricity annually, which amounts to between 3.6 and 6.2 percent of all electricity worldwide. Considering the energy, the total being, 170 to 307 gigawatts. The more we rely on internet-connected smart devices, the more we demand coal/gas/nuclear-powered energy for the required internet traffic.

Lack of Role Models and Perceived Perception

As the technology cycle develops, this significantly affects our daily lives. Understanding the factors affecting technology adoption, is crucial. Especially regarding women and girls, and must be included, when considering the implementation of innovation strategy of information technology. You can see culturally and economically that the impact of some technology adoption by Black women is very low.

Despite smart homes' innovation and functional advantages. Various factors discourage Black females from adopting them. Consider this: lack of role models, accessibility to social capital spaces, microaggression in the workplace and how they feel. A lack of training opportunities and unequal pay; when you examine these uses, you can accept that they have had an unfair start. So of course, their intention to use new information technologies will be limiting.

When you delve deeper, you will see the negative and positive effects of the perception of technology on usage intentions[78,79]. In particular, Kim et al. (2007) *Technology Adoption Decisions in the Household: a Seven-model*

Comparison[80] reported that technology adoption, maximizes its value and those different values of technology recognized by the adopter, also affected behaviour[81]. They explained the adoption process of the technology. Based on the concept of perceived value, that comprehensively considers both the sacrifices (e.g. technicality, perceived fee) and the benefits (e.g., usefulness, enjoyment) that accompany the use of the technology. The perceived sacrifices of smart home technology, which typically embodies difficult usability, cost burden, uncertainty about controllability, and risk awareness of security and are known, to affect internet usage[82,83].

***Smart Home Adoption: The Impact*[84]**

On the contrary, several studies have identified the effects of positive perceptions of technology on adoption[85,86]. Attitude is a crucial factor affecting the adoption of information technology.[87,88,89] Likewise, as a form of expectation and attitude toward technology. Preference affects the intention to use.[90,91] Positive attitudes and expectations in smart home adoption research, has positively altered the choice to use[92,93,94]. Some studies have also reported the impact of different expectations of the "function" of smart home services on adoption[95]. These studies can demonstrate the type of smart home service, control the effectiveness of factors, influencing the adoption process. Other major reasons are user characteristics, such as age, gender, residential types and experience. The expectations and demands for smart homes vary depending on the user characteristics[96,97,98]. Firstly, there are differences in the perception and needs of smart homes depending on the age of the users[99]. For example, although a smart home can provide a convenient and easy automation system. Most people generally want the system to be under their control, rather than it be fully automated or show a concern about the cost of automation[100,101].

Impact on the Elderly and the Differences

On the other hand, some studies have shown that the elderly, generally respond positively, to most smart devices and sensors, associated with health problems. Especially, in the perception of automation, the elderly commonly show a positive attitude[102,103,104]. Many studies have focussed on gender differences. A study by Yang et al. (2017)[105] showed that females had greater intentions, to use smart home services, more than males[106]. Shin et al. (2018)[107] revealed that, the effect of factors affecting smart home adoption (e.g. perceived usefulness and compatibility) varies by gender. Furthermore[108], Nikou (2019)[109] also found that females are more impacted by perceived costs in the smart home adoption process, compared to males[110]. It has validated differences in the level of education in some studies, which highlights the fact that, users with higher education, are more conscientious about the usefulness and benefits of innovative technologies.

Likewise, Shin et al. (2018) found differences between groups with high education levels and those with low expectations and adoption of smart home devices. However, the impact of income levels presents a bone of contention in this field of study. The cost burden of the initial purchase installation and maintenance of smart home services is a significant barrier to adopting the services[111,112]. In particular, the cost burden, caused by the structural changes in the space required, for using new services. Has been one factor, hindering smart home adoption[113]. For instance, Kim et al. (2017)[114] "Who will be smart home users"? An analysis of adoption, and diffusion of smart homes, revealed the users' perception of structural and technical. Buildings 2021, 11, 393 4 of 17 infrastructure, must be prepared, before using smart home services. As it has, a significant impact on the adoption of the services[115]. Overall, the cost burden is a crucial factor in adoption.

Impact on Income Levels

Interestingly, the impact of income levels on the adoption of smart homes, has been supported by very few studies. For example, Yang et al. (2017)[116]suggested that it did not directly link income levels to the adoption of smart homes, as there was no actual effect[117]. Shin et al. (2018)[118] found an indirect result of income levels, but it did not reach statistical significance.

Additionally, smart home adoption is also affected by the type of housing (e.g., flat/general home) where the users currently reside. Some studies show that the needs and intention to use smart home services vary, depending on the type of housing the respondents lived in.[119,120] The researchers speculated that the difference might be, because of different levels of infrastructure, depending on the type of housing. Finally, technology adoption can be persuaded by users' personal lived experiences[121,122,123]. Shih and Veatesh (2004)[124] emphasized the effects of experience as one of the factors that accelerated the diffusion of innovations[125]. In the context of a smart home, likewise, some studies have confirmed, that the user's relevant experiences, affect the expectations and adoption of smart home services[126,127]. Overall, studies on smart home adoption, suggested that several cognitive factors sway users' decisions to adopt smart homes. The decision process may vary, depending on the user's charactcristics and background conditions. Once, given the opportunity. Black women can lead the charge, in using their talents, to tackle the climate crisis. Including, healthcare disparities, advances in tech, and other STEM problems. It is up to companies to recruit, support, keep, and offer equitable pay, to Black women, to further advance and enhance society.

Chapter 5 - How STEM Interacts with the Environment

STEM education plays a vital role in saving the environment, by raising awareness and teaching individuals' various ways to protect their natural habitat. The solutions to climate change need STEM but also must rely on social activism and behavioural change for collaboration with individuals working together. It would be good to explain climate change and understand its impact on our Earth, then we can discuss how to educate females by including them in STEM to help climate change.

What is Climate Change?

Climate change refers to the long-term shifts in temperature and weather patterns. These shifts may be natural. But since the 1800s, human activity has been the main driver. This is primarily due, to the burning of fossil fuels (like coal, oil, and gas) that produce and increase heat-trapping greenhouse gases - a mixture of water, carbon dioxide, and methane. *The 'greenhouse effect' is a process that occurs when gases in the Earth's atmosphere trap the Sun's heat.* This process makes the Earth much warmer than it would be without an atmosphere. The effect is one of the things that makes the Earth a comfortable place to live. The planet needs just the right temperature for living things to survive, but human activity such as the burning of fossil fuels releases excessive carbon dioxide into the atmosphere.

It is estimated that the global surface temperature has increased by 0.14F (0.08C) per decade since 1880, and the rate of warming over the past 40 years is more than twice than 0.32F (0.18C) per decade since 1981[128,129].

Other changes include:

- the warming of the ocean.

- the rise in sea levels.

- and the decrease in snow and ice cover in the Northern Hemisphere, due to the decline in sea ice in the Arctic.

So, if emissions continue to go unchecked, then a further rise will occur until the end of this 21st Century[130] If it does, and if our behaviour does not change, there will be profound implications for humans, society, and the natural world. We must consciously do better to help improve our environment, like recycling, reducing the amount of electricity we use, growing our own food, and buying responsibly.

How do we educate women and girls to help raise climate change awareness?

Whilst doing some work in Ghana, there was the opportunity to plan the #BeMedigitalinclusion climate change hackathon. We wanted to empower women and girls to use their design thinking skills. Also, to inspire them about what women had done in the past, and the challenges they faced, when solving climate change.

An amateur scientist, Eunice Newton Foote's paper, "Circumstances Affecting the Heat of the Sun's Rays" [131] described her experiment comparing two glass cylinders. One filled with CO_2 and the other with moist air, as they sat in the sun. Her discovery was that the CO_2-filled cylinder, became much hotter than the other. The basis for understanding the greenhouse gas effect and its potential, to produce climate change. Foote wrote, *"An atmosphere of that gas would give to our earth, a high temperature; and if at one period of its history, the air had mixed with it a larger proportion than at present, an increased temperature from its action, as well as from increased weight, must have necessarily resulted."*

So, can you see how powerful we women are? Just look at the simple process of understanding the greenhouse effect. Yet even today, women scientists continue to face inequitable access to resources and opportunity. Although, still under-represented in their fields, including climate science. This lack of gender diversity, shapes which possible **scientific questions** get answered — and which ones don't. For instance, if men are the ones answering the questions, then the outcome could have implications for women worldwide, who face unique challenges from climate change.

I say this, although Eunice Newton Foote's work was a hit. It is the Irish physicist, John Tyndall, who discovered the greenhouse gas effect, three years later and who is considered the "founding father" of climate change science. As a recognized scientist, Tyndall had access to more resources and stronger connections to the predominantly male network of scientists, than Foote and was thus better able to deepen and expand his research.

And this inequality continues today[132].

Fewer Women in Science

According to USI data,[133] 30% of the world's researchers are women, with fewer holding senior positions. In addition, a 2019 Lancet report shows how women face further discrimination in STEM[134]. The list is just endless, with the systematic and institutional barriers to women in science. They have less success in winning grant funding, hold fewer positions in academic publishing, and author papers less often. They also face outright discrimination.

This Report on 'How Women in STEM' Face tremendous disadvantages,[135] showed that in considering equally qualified male and female applicants for an academic, managerial position. Both male and female science faculty members, evaluated male applicants more highly and gave them preferential treatment. The men were rated more competent and hireable than female applicants and were offered higher salaries and more career mentoring.

Furthermore, in *challenging and coping strategies experienced by female scientists*[136]. This study found that women faced additional challenges. 24% of 263 female scientists polled. Endured workplace sexual harassment, 71.5% met work-related stress, and 46% experienced work-life imbalance. These results indicated how shocking it is and that there's work to be done in eliminating these unconscious and unrealistic biases. Another study[137] cited that women scientists with children were particularly hard hit by the pandemic, and lost research time.

So, there are constant barriers, inequalities, and specific obstacles that women face. Hence, it helps to understand why there are only 122 women on The Reuters Hot List[138] of the worlds 1,000 top climate scientists. Among the top, 100[139] scientific papers in the last five years, women authored less than half, with only 12 articles having lead authors. Writing this, hurts to the core and makes me very nervous for the future of work, for our women. Hence, I will continue to champion the Global #BeMedigitalinclusion program to ensure that one million females' aspirations are raised in STEM | AI-related careers. The #BeMedigitalinclusion program is developing a gender plan to increase these numbers. By providing equal opportunities for participation and leadership. A gender-inclusive environment, equity, diversity, belonging, more training and guidance to raise awareness.

Why does the #BeMedigitalinclusion program matter for climate science?

Well, as you can see, the impact of climate change has worsened conditions for females, worldwide, and is continuing to decline. Unfortunately, climate change is a threat multiplier, and exacerbating conditions for vulnerable populations. Women are, often, the most vulnerable because they make up 70%[140] of the world's poor. Females suffer the most from the direct and indirect effects of climate change. Since, they have less access to resources, education, and decision-making power, than men, and are frequently the most dependent on natural resources, for their livelihood.

In my time in Ghana, I can see first-hand that Female Farmers, are responsible for 45% to 80% of food production. Yet, continue to be a denied land rights. They are also often prevented from borrowing money (mainly because of the ICT infrastructure). Enabling them to access skills training, fertilizer, better seeds, and the tools that would help increase their crop yields. According to the UN Food and Agriculture Organization,[141] if women had the same access to resources as men, they could raise their results by 20% to 30%. These Ghanaian women are just exceptional, and if one lived in a utopian world, imagine what life would be like if they had access to these fantastic resources? In the rural communities, young females fetch water for cooking, cleaning, and gardens and wood for fuel. Together with the rise in climate change and the resulting droughts, floods, and heatwaves. These tasks are becoming more complex and time-consuming, leaving females less time to pursue their education, careers, and other sources of income, thus impacting on their mental and emotional health.

When climate change affects food supplies and causes food shortages, it disproportionately, impacts the health of females, more so, than that of men. Besides, the economic stress caused, it can also mean, less money for medication. For example, where pregnant women are overlooked for the care, they need. This adds more emotional stress, than is necessary. Not only that, but more women than men, die in natural disasters[142] as they have fewer savings, and properties to deal with. Thus, having no alternative, but to shelter in unsafe places. This lack of assets and restrictions on their human rights, may also prevent them from moving to safer locations.

I personally, believe that increasing the pipeline of female climate scientists, could create better understanding and provide more solutions for some of these, far-reaching implications of climate change.

How will the #BeMedigitalinclusion of female climate change scientists, offer a different perspective?

From my personal experience and wider connections, I believe women are better collaborators. Especially in negotiation, as they are, more responsive to the vulnerable, and to a greater extent, more sensitive to nature. My time in Ghana, has given me access to women at the grassroots level, making a positive impact. These foundations are vital for females seated at the table, because they are the ones, who can give an accurate account, of what's happening on the ground level. Women tend to have stronger emotional intelligence and show resilience, where this can have a positive influence, during the strategic planning stages. Palaeoclimatologist Maureen Raymo, Co-founder of, *Dean of the Columbia Climate School* and *Director of the Lamont-Doherty Earth Observatory.* - Acknowledges there are no fundamental differences between scientists, based on gender,[143,] and we must move on from, hiring females and minorities, to improving group dynamics. Now is the time to hire a person, where everyone has a shot at being their best self. Bringing their brilliant ideas and unique perspectives to the table. Equally, employing a healthy workforce, with the desirable dynamics, is everyone's responsibility—we all need to do the work of making sure diverse perspectives come together, in collaborative and productive ways. Educated females can run and grow a sustainable business, especially climate-smart agriculture. They can inspire community action, to build climate resilience, innovate green technologies, and lead local and global policies that change the status quo.

Ghana has also given me a new perspective, where I had the opportunity to travel throughout the different regions. The females I met, came with more life differing experiences and backgrounds, that can improve climate science because everyone brings a different perspective.

This diversity of lived experiences, leads to further research questions that the #BeMedigitalinclusion program addresses. So, having different backgrounds and observing a diverse community, can spark research questions, that wouldn't get asked if we were sitting behind our computers. So being on the ground level, helps us to, identifying females, at the grassroots of climate change solutions.

What the future looks like for STEM in the Environment?

The climate is undoubtedly changing and, I will address the what, the how, and the impact, it will have on our lives in the future.

Academy to Global Footprint Network–a non-profit that calculates how we manage the world's resources via Earth Overshoot Day. In 2021, it shows that we used up one year's amount of resources like water, to produce food, clothes, and everything else, in only seven months[144]. We need more female experts in STEM to be part of the solution, since biotechnologists can save countless lives with Covid-19 vaccines, for example. The role as an engineer, will help to lessen the ill-effects of the build-up of CO_2. As most females are good at maths, and advise policymakers on the likelihood of floods, heatwaves, and other weather changes. So, they can plan accordingly; the impact is immense, if not immeasurable.

There is a need to take a diverse approach to bridging a gendered skill gap, that will help to reach climate goals. As closing the gender gap is still an issue, as STEM roles are still heavily dominated by men. The data shows that globally 72% of scientific researchers are males, and just one in five countries has achieved gender parity[145].

This inequality begins in schools, where girls may be diverted away from science and maths subjects[146], before it spills into the real world. Data from the United Nations Educational, Scientific and Cultural Organization[147] shows only 30% of female students take up STEM-related fields, in higher education.

From my personal lived and work experiences, I have seen first-hand, where gender equity in STEM is a very important step to take[148]. Having a more equal playing field for females, could help narrow the skills gap, by increasing employment. Including, productivity of women, and reduce occupational segregation. I feel that empowering more women in STEM, will disrupt the cycle of poverty in underserved communities. In which, females rarely have access to the same opportunities as men[149]. Considering, a broad and diverse workforce, is critical, if we are to tackle the climate crisis collectively. This being the biggest challenge, facing not only the scientific world, but the entire planet.

Time is running out! Climate change will have a detrimental impact on the future, if we do not act now! The #BeMedigitalinclusion program is working with scientists and practitioners to design and create a diverse range of solutions inspired by lived experiences. Our #BeMedigitalinclusion females have been involved, by helping us to analyse the problem. Also assisting us to formulate the research questions, piloting of solutions and community engagement.

Chapter 6–Case Studies
Microaggressions v. Macroaggressions

Microaggressions can be around race or gender. Gender microaggressions include sexual objectification, the use of sexist language, making assumptions based on gender. The use of sexist humour, slights, insults, or using a derogatory analogy. Some of these subtle and not-so-subtle actions or comments, may not seem like a big deal, and one incident in isolation, may not be. But, in reality, these incidents inhibit women from doing their best work, by being optimally productive and instead, undermining their success. Women, particularly Black women, cite these disrespectful, sometimes, toxic behaviours, as one factor, influencing their decisions to leave a job. When they mention these actions that lead to a reluctant decision to quit, that they otherwise want to stay in. They describe it as *"death by a thousand cuts"*. A steady diet of microaggression, disconnects and wears people down.

Macroaggression occurs on a systemic level—for instance, unequal pay practices, or conditions for a particular group of people, especially Black people. In contrast, microaggressions are intentional or unintentional, verbal or non-verbal behaviours, that occur in everyday interactions. They are often unacknowledged, and casually degrade, demean, or put down someone who is part of a group (for instance, a gender, race, or ethnic group). According to this research, 64% of women are exposed to this form of discrimination, with non-white women experiencing it, more than anyone else.

Case Study 1

I hated leaving my one-month-old baby, but needed to work, since money was tight. My first banking job was in a financial institution on Lombard Street, London. Where I travelled from New Cross to London Bridge, thirty-five minutes, door to door. It was a traumatic time for me, as I had a child to feed and bills to pay, and there was only one income coming in. Therefore, it was my responsibility to ensure, I cared for the household.

Even though I felt accountable, I did not feel safe, and whenever I entered the building, I thought I was not good enough or welcomed. I noticed I would "code-switch" whenever I was at work, because I began to embrace my co-worker's culture. Then, only switching to my authentic self, whenever I was at home, around family and friends. Eventually, I passed my three-month probation and became a permanent staff member.

One day, I made a mistake when given a task, and my supervisor, Mr Welsh, told me off. He harassed me, whenever I was ready to hand in my completed assignments. He would interrogate and humiliate me in front of my peers, leaving me helpless. In one instance, the manager called me into the office and told me I was not fit for purpose. I was like: "*What! No way, I am not hanging around to be traumatized by this experience*". So, I left! This harmful treatment negatively affected my mental health, and I struggled to deal with these problematic workplace treatments.

It affected me so much that I had difficulty completing my work on time. I wanted to be liked by my managers, so much that I wore weaves, dressed and talked in a particular way. But honestly, I was never fond of the lie I was living. At the time, I did not fully comprehend what was happening to me, but as I grew older, it became clearer. As a young mum, I knew this unjust treatment was incorrect and armed with this knowledge; I approached an organization that dealt with harassment in the workplace. Eventually, I executed a grievance and took legal steps that led to the bank's solicitor contacting me, and on behalf of the bank, they offered me £1,500. I agreed and signed a non-disclosure document that would not mention the bank's name if my treatment came to light. At the time, I did not totally understand the process and realized too late, that I could have received a considerable sum, had I not accepted. Within the confines of that workplace, instances of racism, homophobia, sexism, and other biases appeared, and the treatment received, was just distasteful.

Most of the employees were Black women, all doing data entry work. I never understood why, since there was no mental stimulation, as far as I knew. I was like, "*I'm a problem solver and needed to do more*". That environment felt like a factory with a conveyor belt, with its repetitive tasks. I knew one thing; this environment was not for me.

Case Study 2

I worked for an international bank in Moorgate, Finsbury Circus. My boss was a white man with the weirdest name (a named part of the body). At the same time, my confidence was suffering, because of my previous experience, and I feared this man, since he made me feel stupid. He checked my work and would humiliate me, if there was an error. He behaved, as if he was superior to me. In turn, I would check and recheck all the codes I wrote, before I sent them to him. I always ensured my work was one hundred percent accurate. Yet, he never complimented me, on my precision. Instead, where I should have received a pay increase. The unrealistic targets and up to a point, I feel I gave him, so much of my power. Unfortunately, as a result, I became sick, due to the mental stress, but wouldn't give up. I'd still go to work every day and do my job, to the best of my ability.

One day, I was making swift payments and noticed significant transactions going through, that were suspicious. I told him, and the bank managers, that something was incorrect; they took action and thwarted the transactions. I saved the bank hundreds of thousands of pounds, and, without recognition for this. Instead, my response to that was, *"are you serious"*? Despite other challenges outside of work (family drama - another book!) I was getting better at my job; I was so good, that my manager, kept getting upset.

To stay motivated and inspired. I established a reflection time to read Iyanla Vanzant's '*Acts of Faith*: daily devotions for spiritual growth', '*One Day My Soul Just Opened Up*' and '*In the Meantime*'. These books helped build my confidence and emotional well-being, to move forward and step in faith. I went to an employment agency, with that knowledge and dissatisfaction with work. There, the agency rep told me that my skills, experience, and qualifications, could get me £35,000 per year, more than I was getting. I asked what I needed to do to make it a reality, and he said I needed to provide an updated CV, and he would do the rest. I had, and he did.

Eventually, I secured an interview at Coutts and Co - a leading international bank. The recruitment manager was so impressed with the voluntary *work,* that she gave me the role on the spot. She said: *"You have a child. You're a single parent mother and giving back to your community and more. You're just exceptional."* I was like, *"I know"*, but I did not brag about it! Unfortunately, I could not take the job, because of childcare issues beyond my control. But, the next day, I got another opportunity, at another institution that fit my situation.

At Finsbury Circle, the harassment, and victimization made me feel worthless. The unfair treatment exposed me to subtle racism, that affected my physical and mental health. In the workplace, many Black women still experience these behaviours, that result in health disparities. Such as, being disproportionately at greater risk of stroke, cognitive decline, and neurodegenerative disorders (for instance, Alzheimer's disease, compared to their white counterparts).

Case Study 3

This bank was more prestigious. The glass building had a corporate look and made me feel like I had arrived. But, again, the treatment I received was horrible. I remember on two occasions, as a senior member at a meeting with a potential partner, who ignored me. He shook hands with my white male subordinates because they assumed that I was the analyst, and the other, was the leader.

The woman who managed me, disliked the agency paying me more, so she bullied, victimized and harassed me. They labelled me too aggressive. I challenged this and complained to the Head of Services and HR, telling them I did not appreciate the treatment received, and that if it continued, I would take it further. The same manager wanted to get me back. So once, Sarah, my supervisor at the time, complained to HR that I failed to complete a task correctly, which I had. To get back at me, they ensured I stayed behind, before allowing me to leave, knowing I had a child. Another time, they made it difficult for me to take my child to the hospital, by delaying me with tasks. I was so angry, and working with them was so hard.

Interestingly, I knew this was unfair treatment at work, was unacceptable, at the tender age, of twenty-one years old. The strain was too much, and being a single parent, I knew my child felt my stress. I did not want that. I needed to be in an environment where I could achieve and add value. So, I resigned. Whenever I did my reflec*tion* moments, I read those Iyanla books and was like: *"OMG! I can't keep losing my job because these white chicks don't like me.* It is boring!"

At this point, I said enough was enough, because the private sector, was horrendous for me. So, I decided to switch my career and enter the public sector. But I was only jumping from the frying pan, straight into the fire!

Case Study 4

My situation was affecting my daughter. She was losing out on me not being fully present, and unfortunately, her school grades dropped. Although my child struggled, I offered to volunteer at her school, since I had read that, literacy, numeracy, and ICT were concerning issues there. According to the primary school league table, the entire school was failing. So, I took action, and decided to speak to the head teacher. I wrote a letter explaining who I was, and what I could do to help improve the student's attainment levels. The Headteacher called me at home, inviting me to do, whatever I needed, in the school. As a result of that favourable decision, I set up a parent ICT group, establishing '*Academy Achievers*'. For me, this was a 'win-win'. I could support my child, her friends, and their parents in Literacy, Numeracy, and ICT. In creating this time, assisted me in getting involved, as a youth leader and leading the ICT after-school club in Deptford.

Eventually, I completed my Post Graduate Certificate in Education (PGCE) in Computing/Information Communication Technology at St Mary's University. Including my Master's, in Information Communication Technology. I then, became my daughter's Computer Science/ICT teacher, establishing the '*Academy Achievers*', as a Saturday School.

Although, entering the UK educational system, was a bittersweet moment for me. First, I taught young people about computer science, which was awesome. Soon afterwards, I got the opportunity to develop myself, by buying books and attending courses, to ensure I was ready to deliver. It was just a pleasant experience, seeing those young faces in the classroom, where I would be responsible for their learning. So, by the time the end of the year arrived, I could write a report on their educational attainment. The student's response - *"We had so much fun in Miss Watson's class"*.

Macro Aggression:

It was from the senior leadership team, where the discrimination and trauma came from. Although I had it under control, the academic, classroom behaviour, and subject knowledge. There was a real challenge with the leadership team. I was not fond of the excessive workload I received, but with my digital skills, I knew how to work smarter. I learned Python, to build a script to calculate my Key Stage 3, 4 and 5 grades, using Panda. The script was quick and able to calculate and provide each student a grade accurately; this reduced my planning and marking time considerably. It was a game-changer.

The stress begins, with dealing with pay gaps, wealth gaps, educational attainment gaps, and lack of investment in our schools.

(I have used the names of areas to protect the schools that I taught at. However, I will mention the names of the schools, where I got the most enjoyment and development from).

Rotherhithe

When I began my first teaching job, I never knew how stressful it would be, because I lived quite a distance away. Yet, I would drop my daughter at her nursery at 5:30 am and every morning I would travel to Uxbridge, returning to Lewisham by 8 pm, to pick her up. My placement was traumatic. My mentor, a white man, was the person I reported to, for anything related to teaching and learning. He was always late, could not spell and was not fit for purpose, in leading young people and preparing them for the future of work. I disliked him, because he was always ill-prepared and smelt of alcohol and cigarettes. He disliked me, was rude, and never marked, any of the student's work. His pedagogical practices were questionable too. How he carried himself to school, demonstrated that he had no regard for the students.

I, however, would get up at 5 am, prepare my child's meals, get her ready, and then take her to her nanny, who would drop her off at nursery. As I would, often leave too early arriving at school at 7:30 am to prepare. As part of the (PGCE) Post Graduate Certificate in Education course, which composed of my teaching portfolio. I was so focused and showed up! I took my role seriously, by planning and preparing my lessons, and the coaching and support from Queen Mary University. Roger, the PGCE Lead, did not match what I saw at the school.

As well as dealing with my mentor's inadequacies, I had issues with the Head of ICT. When I first met her, I was like: *"Yes, there's a woman in middle management"*. I could learn so much from her, but unfortunately, this was not the case. She was an Asian woman, and her behaviour and attitude, implied that she felt, she was better than me. I remember, when Ofsted called the school, to say they were coming the next day. The Headteacher selected my A-level computing lesson to be observed, (because of my achievements); I was so excited and honoured to be chosen.

The next day, I saw, from across my classroom, that the Ofsted members, were with some non-Black teachers and leaders.

I was so ecstatic, that I would get to meet the Inspectors so, I could showcase my work and students to them. But the Head of ICT at the time, was giving the members a tour, and passed my classroom, while avoiding eye contact with me. I could not believe this–I wanted them to come and see the students. The Head of ICT made no effort to talk or say hello to me, even though I made it my duty to do so. I remember one day, I was doing some work in the office, and she entered, sat down and ignored me. I was in disbelief.

Not only that, but I noticed that she would use her best friend, who was my, then, supervisor, and someone I did not like. She would allow him to yell at me in front of colleagues and my students, when I made mistakes, and he would also hover over my desk.

As time passed, it started to feel like she was looking for any mistake to provoke my supervisor to berate me, in front of my colleagues. When I asked her for help or information, that was a part of the company policy, her response was, *"You should know this already."* One of the worst days played out like this, when she came to my classroom with her arms crossed and scolded me for a mistake, my supervisor made. He was her best friend, and he forgot to fill me in, on one extra step. The entire department saw what happened, and my white colleagues didn't come to my rescue, nor did they try to make me feel better about the workplace harassment.

I had to report to my university about my experience, as a student teacher. It became apparent she did not like me and wanted me to leave. She, and my supervisor, decided to make things difficult for me. Her attitude was appalling, and she used her position of power to bully, harass and victimize me. I felt vulnerable. I told my supervisor at St Mary's University, what was happening, and he was concerned. He said I was his liveliest student-teacher, who always got the work done and after his observations, he thought I would be a fantastic teacher. His best student-teacher, enthusiastic, punctual and prompt. He, even, advised me to discuss my treatment with the senior leadership team.

So, I had a good conversation with the Director at the school and stated what I wanted to achieve. He approved and said he would support me. After leaving that meeting, I still felt uncomfortable, so I requested a transfer to another school. I ended up, at Ernest Bevin College, one of the best schools I ever taught at and will never forget.

Tooting BEC

I drove to school, and taught GCSE and A Level Computing in my first year, doing exceptionally well. The first day I arrived at the school, the staff room was busy with many teachers rushing in and out–this is awesome! The department head, a white lady, was about to retire. She told me my lessons were outstanding, but she could not write this on my annual report, as there was no room for improvement! And so, she graded me with a 'Good'. I was annoyed, since I expected a better grade for working so hard. While growing up, my father always told me I needed to work twice as hard as a white child, and I remember saying to him: "So if I get an A and a white child gets a C, are you saying that we are on par?" He had said, not exactly, but that's how it would seem. So, when this woman gave me 'Good', I knew my lessons were the best, but knew why she graded me the way she had. It did not sit well with me, but I knew she was leaving by the end of term, and I could not care less.

I later worked alongside the Headteacher and loved our lessons. He was lovely and worked in the computing department with four other white men. We had a blast! They were easy-going, allowing me to teach and introduce new concepts in technology. I was able to lead the PGCE training of new teachers, and my lessons were always outstanding. The experience I had at this school was so unique. I had just completed my Master's in ICT, and the support I received from the administration was terrific. I used my Year 9 students to write about a virtual reality classroom, and they needed to pretend they were avatars in space. They thought I was crazy, but we had fun.

While there, I applied for an opportunity to go to South Africa for a teaching exchange. So, I wrote an application and won. The application was outstanding, but I still needed to meet the criteria. The Headteacher said my application stuck out because the word 'ubiquitous computing' intrigued him. He wanted to see how I would develop that concept in South Africa. Unfortunately, due to still being a student teacher in training, I still needed to receive my teaching registration number the following month, which meant I missed out in going to South Africa. I was devastated! My entire department couldn't believe it. I learned a good lesson and made sure from now on; I would make sure that anything I applied for, I fully met the eligibility criteria.

In my first year, I got promoted to Key Stage 3 Computer Science Coordinator and supported PGCE students. I enjoyed every teaching moment, since the young boys were achieving so much. I remember a time in my first year of education, when the boys were predicted to attain Es and Fs, but they eventually achieved Cs in my ICT class. So, with the continued GCSE results, I wanted more for my career. My child would start secondary school within a year, so I wanted her to attend a good school in Lewisham. A position came up for a Lewisham school for Head of ICT and E-learning. I was determined to apply, and hopefully, when I secured it, my daughter could start school there. Fortunately for me, this happened. I got the job, and my daughter attended the school. It was a dream come true.

South East London

As Head of ICT and E-learning at the school, I was so proud to be teaching my daughter. She saw me every day for five years. I was her role model at both school and home. She had the best of both worlds, mummy at home and Miss Watson at school. I remember when she used to get it wrong and call me mum in the classroom! I would give her a look, and she would quickly correct herself. Bless her.

After finishing my ICT Master's degree, I met with my new Headteacher, weekly. Our school led the *'Building School for the Future Programme'*, where, about fifteen schools went through a makeover, with contemporary facilities, like a sports hall, drama studios, kitchen, dining hall. In addition to a Science, Technology, Engineering, and Maths block, being constructed. I led the entire borough's ICT infrastructure, by assisting in developing the ICT curriculum and teacher training, on a virtual E-learning portal (called Frontal). This role was instrumental in gaining my Non-Executive Director Role within the same borough.

This school was very special to me; I was fond of the Headteacher from South Africa and had access to her like nobody else. I saw what she did, how she wrote, the books she read, and the talks she did. She was such an inspiration, *'simply the best, better than all the rest'*! I could advise her on new and emerging technologies; she was my role model, since I learned everything from her. Not only that, but I admired her and aspired to be a high achiever, because of her.

She, Disrupts

My subject knowledge and tech experience added value to the school's development. Still, unfortunately, our professional relationship ended, because most of the other teachers and leaders were apprehensive about her. She was a no-nonsense woman, with high expectations and held everybody to account and I noticed how I was treated differently. Furthermore, I had the upper hand, because I knew everything about the school. So, when it came to being called to the Headteacher's office, after Mr Bill complained about me being sick. Even checking on all my lesson plans and cover work meticulously, although I had documented everything. My case was closed. I had come prepared. Later, I wanted to complete my MBA and The Headteacher, who had an MBA herself, advised me not to do it, because I was too young. I left during the summer term, which was not the best thing to do, because my students needed me, but I had no choice. As a result, I got another job as Head of Faculty at another school.

During the interview, the new Headteacher told me it was terrific, but the reference they received from my current

Headteacher was concerning. I requested a copy and was so distraught, when I read it. I decided, to challenge my current Headteacher, and asked what reason she had, for giving me such a lousy reference. I had done everything right, and my results were exceptional year after year. My punctuality and attendance were good and, I realized that my current Headteacher was unhappy I was leaving, and discovered, she was using her powers, to try to stop me. It did not work, though; I had another plan!

In my last conversation with her, she said, *"Paulette, you're like dynamite, ready to explode, and when you do, it'll be everywhere"*. I had no idea what she was on about. But I do now!

West London Microaggression

From 2008 onwards, the microaggression I experienced within the British educational system intensified, until 2014, I had enough.

After leaving my daughter's school in 2008, I decided my next role would be temporary, and the next day, there was an invitation to attend an interview at a school in

West London. It was an academy. I did not have a clue about these schools and were about to have a rude awakening. The interview went well. I had a lesson on 'Databases', and then the students interviewed me. The staff and students loved me, and I knew this, because of the feedback from the interview I received. Eventually, I became Head of Faculty–ICT |Business Studies | Health and Social Care. I was only there for one year, since I was very strategic with my exit plan. I was completing my Executive MBA and planned to enter leadership or start my entrepreneurial tech start-up global journey. When I realized I got the job in West London, I wrote to the Headteacher - a white male, requesting a meeting, to which he agreed. I handed him a letter explaining I needed Fridays off. So, I could complete my Executive MBA part-time course at the Institute of Education and would like the school to finance it. My boldness impressed him, and he said yes and agreed to pay and give me the Fridays off. It was sealed and delivered in writing the next day. But ten days later, he left.

I was shocked! The new Headteacher was a white woman, the school's previous consultant. Thankfully, everything was sorted, before she could play any part in my professional development, because, as soon as she became Headteacher, she started bullying me. She observed me every week, with unrealistic targets, and then gave me satisfactory. Then, over a period of three to six months, I endured this woman observing my lessons every week, but when she did, I was satisfied with my excellent subject knowledge–if I do say so myself.

At first, I took every feedback on board and even taught my students, who were attaining top grades. My lesson observations needed to reflect the results. A good or exceptional mark was all that mattered, but I couldn't understand why she made it her duty, to keep me from progressing, while she promoted other members, who were mainly, white female staff. At one point, she even demoted me from being '*Head of Faculty*'. Though I was getting this treatment, I still attended university part-time, liaising with other headteachers, while learning. I had access to leadership meetings and seminars and understood more about strategic planning, system leadership, financial planning, and equity of resource allocation. Recognizing the barriers I faced at this school, I handed in my notice, and after that experience, I decided I had enough of full-time teaching.

On reflection, in every school I taught, white women sought to make my life miserable; this was not true for all white men, though. I felt there was no need to "fit" in or adjust who I was, to be accepted, even though, the culture within these schools caused me so much stress and anxiety. So, I guess teaching in schools was not for me.

Black Women in Education

I realized, many Black women experienced microaggressive behaviour in the education system. I experienced the same treatment, in three different schools. However, ten times worse (in comparison) to my white female counterparts. In one particular school, a teacher was ill and took a lot of time off. When he realized, I was teaching his GCSE revision classes and the students were doing well. He decided he wanted to return and cause problems, by not allowing me to teach, as if he was jealous. The students, however, started to enjoy lessons. In another school, my students were the best; I felt the department's head wanted to micromanage me. What was hilarious, she was the so-called Head of the ICT Department. Yet, had no idea about teaching computing - she kept asking me to support her. Whenever I felt the impact of bullying, harassing and victimizing from these people in positions of power, I needed an exit plan.

In another instance, I wanted to apply for a deputy head role, but the Headteacher said no, despite her knowing full well I was more than qualified. She used my CV to place me across the entire school, where I taught all subjects and developed the school curriculum, while teaching all key stages. The school was so annoyed with me when I left. Since they realized they could not replace me, and if I had stayed, I could have helped develop their

ICT strategic infrastructure. For this reason, the school decided to withhold my pay for six months.

Finally!

In my experience of working in the education environment. I have found institutionalized racism is inherent and prevalent. The schools I worked in, may have policies for harassment, bullying and microaggression. However, the schools' culture undermined any written plan or procedure. Although, I made sure that in my career, I qualified in the field I loved and was passionate about. It was enjoyable, being able to turn around students with behavioural challenges, which made others jealous of my success, with the underlying issues, being my interactions with white women.

Eventually, skilled and qualified as I was, I became frustrated and demotivated with having to confront the daily institutionalized racism, harassment, bullying, and ostracization. These reasons, were why, I walked away from full-time education.

I am taking you on a personal journey, to help you understand the real-life challenges I encountered weren't? necessary. To be honest, I am 100% certain, that there are other stories experienced by Black women, which are too horrific to go through right now. Yet still they Rise!

Despite all my qualifications, work experiences, knowledge within the Tech sector. The personal life barriers were real.

In these case studies, I only focused on my work experiences. I did not share about my housing, pay, wealth, and health inequalities–However, I will share another time.

I wanted you to fully understand the biases I was experiencing at work. Not only that, but I know that bias is neurological. It fascinates me how the brain works. For me, this is really my concern, when it comes to AI tools, and how the unconscious and unrealistic biases, will be played out, when designing these codes. Will history repeat itself under the algorithmic unconscious codes? Covid-19 has affected so many Black women and left many of us displaced. It has been a journey where we have lost loved ones, lost our jobs and earnings.

Chapter 7–COVID-19

Writing this chapter, I will draw on the 4th and 5th Sustainable Development Goals — quality education and gender equality. Using the lens of intersectionality, I will discuss race, gender, ethnicity, religion, and socioeconomic to understand diversity and socially include other women in this space. In the same vein, representation to achieve gender equality in the education system, means recognizing the persistent gaps in equity and equal opportunities for all genders or underrepresented groups. So, it starts here and now! Covid-19 has disproportionately affected women and girls globally on several fronts. Relating directly to SDG 5 Gender equality (SDG) 5 - Gender equality, which focuses on empowering women and girls and linking other SDGs.

Global data[150] reveals that 70% of frontline workers are women and girls (including midwives, nurses, and community health workers)[151]. In these positions, infection rates are three times higher for women than for their male counterparts[152]. And yet, the global gender pay gap in the health sector is approximately 28%, which is higher than the overall gender pay gap at 16%[153]. Women's participation in the labour force has also hit record-low levels in certain countries. Severely impacted by the closures of schools and nursery centres. For example, the U.S. has experienced its lowest for 33 years[154]. In the U.S., 2.3m women have left the workforce over the past year, compared to 1.8m men[155].

There has also been a gendered impact of the pandemic on poverty rates. There is a high number of people in poverty owing to the pandemic, which will have severe implications on SDG 1, and seeks to eradicate poverty, in all forms, everywhere.

According to the United Nations Development Programme (UNDP), compared to the original 2021 forecasts. There will be 47m women and girls, pushed into extreme poverty because of Covid-19. 435m. Women and girls will live on less than $1.90 daily. Reversing the positive downward trajectory of extreme poverty in women and girls, before the pandemic[156]. Therefore, the gender poverty gap will widen, especially in the 25 to 34-year-old age group[157]. In 2021, for every 100 men living in poverty, there were 118 women[158]. By 2030, this gap will widen to 121 women for every 100 men[159,160].

Social infrastructure is also critical for gender equity: in 80% of households that lack on-site water. Women, and girls, are obligated to collect water for the household[161]. Not only does this reveal the gendered effects of infrastructure and the intersection with SDG 6: water and sanitation. But it also shows the increased exposure and vulnerability of those women who lack this critical infrastructure and are collecting essentials.

SDG 4 Education, which seeks to close the socioeconomic gaps in access to education, has been one of the most severe setbacks. School closures because of Covid-19, have impacted 91% of learners worldwide.[162]

Keeping girls in the picture is likely to result in many girls never returning to school. UNESCO estimates that, 11m girls and young women are at risk of dropping out of education in the next year[163] because of the pandemic's economic impact alone. 130m girls were already out of school, according to the agency[164]. The Malala Fund estimates that 20m more secondary school-aged girls could remain out of the classroom, long after the coronavirus pandemic has passed. Based upon the experiences of the Ebola epidemic in Sierra Leone[165].

There is also a disparity in whether online learning has occurred. The digital gap is widening, with an Action Aid survey of 1,219 women aged 18 to 30 in the urban areas of India, Ghana, Kenya, and South Africa. This showing that only about 22% of those who were studying said they could continue their education remotely at 17. This disparity is likely to have extreme consequences on the development of our next generation of women. As, just three months of missed schooling can result in 1.5 years of learning loss years later at 18. But girls lose more than education when schools are closed. They become increasingly at risk of sexual abuse, child marriage, forced labour, malnutrition, teen pregnancy, forced marriage, and violence.

A World Bank report, released in partnership with the Malala Fund in 2018, shows that limited educational opportunities for women and girls who complete secondary school, could cost the global economy between $15trn and $30trn. This economic stress is likely to affect local and international economies, severely. A recent report indicates that two-thirds of poorer countries have decreased education budgets since Covid-19 began. This was because of fiscal constraints, likely to increase, the already high barriers to entry for girls, wanting to access education.

I will be looking at Ghana and the United States (I had already focussed on Jamaica) - in an article called *Every Click Matters*; School Leadership in the Caribbean: *Perceptions, Practices, Paradigms*. I will also draw from that chapter to illustrate my point.

Chapter 8 - Overview: GHANA

Ghana is a middle-income country, in the Atlantic Ocean, bordered by Togo, Côte d'Ivoire, and Burkina Faso. The population is around 30m, of which, 49% are women. It is a diverse politically, economically, ethnically, and demographical country. The main social and economic divides are between the country's north, south, urban and rural areas. These dividers, result from ecological conditions and inequalities in service delivery, driven by geography and the country's colonial history. Previously, the northern region was used as a labour reserve for mines and cocoa farms in the south. Resulting in limited investments in education, infrastructure, and economic development for the north.

Ghana has been a notable leader in poverty reduction, on the African continent. However, the country's rapid economic growth was hit hard by the Covid-19 pandemic. So, from 2017 to 2019, the economy grew at an average of 7% annually, before experiencing a sharp contraction, following the pandemic outbreak in early 2020. The economic impact of Covid-19 has had a significant impact on households. They estimate the poverty rate to have increased from 25% in 2019 to 25.5% in 2020. Despite Ghana's positive economic growth, before the Covid-19 pandemic, poverty rates remain higher than 50% in the Northern, Upper East, and Upper West regions, with no change between 2005 and 2016 in the Volta Region. Ghana does not have a national policy for research[166]. Although, it does have a comprehensive policy framework for science, technology, and innovation (STI) (research system in Ghana)[167].

The 2017 National STI Policy, articulates key barriers to innovation. Committing to supporting adopting foreign innovation, as an economic driver. Ghana was ranked 112th out of the 132 economies in the Global Innovation Index (GII) for 2021, slightly improving from 2020 to 2019, ranking 108th and 106th, respectively. Among the 27 economies in sub-Saharan Africa, Ghana ranks 12th. Ghana attained positive scores in four of the seven GII pillars: human capital and research, infrastructure, knowledge, and technology outputs, and creative outputs[168], above average for the sub-Saharan Africa region. Conversely, Ghana scores lower in three pillars: business sophistication, market sophistication, and institutions, with its weakest performance in institutions.

Ghana is a beautiful country, situated in the West region of Africa, and I love it here!

Since being here in 2021, I have become more and more concerned with the need for more Ghanaian women in the Tech scene. These are the gender disparities that are currently facing Ghanaian women.

Low enrolment in STEM programs, compared to their male counterparts. Ghana's women, have long-established low enrolment rates. However, visiting Ghana in 2021 and pitched at the Ghana Education Service; I got a letter, saying that the #BeMedigitalinclusion program can go across Takaradi and Sekondi. I had the opportunity to collaborate with the STEM regional coordinator, to lead the STEM program. Out of the 100 students at the time who attended, only four girls were part of the program; I was so shocked, I wanted to grasp the issues and the reason for the low take. Various factors, including cultural norms, societal expectations, and limited access to educational opportunities, influence the lack of girls in these programs. *I'm like, "are you serious"?* Because, coming from a Jamaican cultural background–although there were moments when our daily household chores were a key responsibility for us girls–it did not stop us or interfere with us pursuing our educational and career goals. In fact, we always got praised and supported financially in whatever we wanted. Another reason for this disparity is the low representation of women in the STEM Workforce.

Ghanaian women's experiences, challenges, and barriers contribute to their under-representation in STEM. Including cultural biases, lack of access to resources, gender stereotypes, and lack of female role models. Another point is the lack of initiatives to promote gender equality in STEM. According to the Ghana Statistical Service, 2021 population. Women make up 48% of the total population. Yet, their representation in STEM occupations was low. Although the Ghanian Government, in collaboration with various organizations, including STEM Academy Achievers Ghana (SAAG). Have been implementing initiatives to encourage and support women's participation and create a safe environment for women to pursue STEM.

Gender Context:[169]

Ghana has also made significant strides in gender equality and women's empowerment at the legislative and policy levels. They have done this in the following ways: International Day of Women and Girls in Science - 11th February 2022.

Education:

Twenty STEM Centres and ten models STEM Senior High Schools, Nationwide - reposition the country, in ensuring equality in STEM Education (Mrs Opare, Director of STEM Services)

Teacher Training:

Patriarchal gender norms, continue to painstakingly influence the rights, freedoms, security, and quality of life that girls and women experience daily. I have struggled with the social beliefs, values, attitudes, and behaviours about the role and entitlement of men and women, which generally dictate that, women are subordinate or inferior. It is crucial, in hindering women's participation in decision-making and lack of representation in political and government positions. Recent studies on the gender context of Ghana, reveal that a weak understanding of gender main streaming in the public sector. Including a lack of effective monitoring and evaluation systems in the Ministry of Gender, Children, and Social Protection (MoG CSP). Significantly constrain the effective implementation of Ghana's national legal frameworks and international commitments on gender equality. I want to address some critical points about gender and social norms, to explain why women are consistently disadvantaged.

Discrimination, Violence, Sexual Harassment, and Exploitation of Women

Gender and social norms in Ghana, often justify and perpetuate various forms of discrimination and violence, including sexual violence. When we consider gender norms related to sex and entitlement for men. This is acceptable, and is not the same for women, who have multiple sex partners. Interestingly, these male partners, often, put these women at risk and are most likely to blame women for HIV acquisition. Women face sexual harassment and exploitation when accessing employment opportunities or public services. The perceptions of an individual from the northern region of Ghana, particularly Northern Muslims, are regarded less capable and face discrimination and limited job opportunities.

Education and Entrepreneurship

Persistent gender gaps, in education and geographical locations, result in poverty. The average number of years of schooling, that the poorest girls, aged 20 to 24, from rural areas in Ghana can attain, is about four years. Compared with a full 13 years, for girls from more affluent homes in urban areas[170]. Gender disparities become more substantial at the secondary and tertiary level, even in the wealthiest households. Gender gaps appear to be the highest between young men and women, at the tertiary education level too. Teaching and learning materials and resources, constitutes proof of significant gender bias, from the primary school level. Reinforcing patriarchal norms and expectations of men as leaders and providers and women as caregivers and domestic helpers[171].

Regarding entrepreneurship, Ghana has one of the world's highest rates of women entrepreneurs. In 2019, Ghana ranked second worldwide for the highest percentage of women's business ownership. Women own close to four in every ten businesses (37.9%); this number declined only marginally, between the 2019 and 2020 indexes. In conjunction with Ghana, now taking third place behind Botswana (2nd place) and Uganda (1st place). While these numbers appear highly promising at first glance, they may also allude to the fact that women face more significant constraints than men, in securing other jobs and formal employment opportunities. Stakeholder interviews, from Ghana, reveal that male business owners sometimes list their wives as registered business owners. Women should be more involved in the company to take advantage of financial and other opportunities for women-led businesses.

Physical infrastructure and government programs help these women thrive, as entrepreneurs or business leaders. Despite the outward markings of progress in this area, women entrepreneurs in Ghana, face further constraints that contribute to significant gender gaps in profits, ranging from 23 to 73%. There are also fewer opportunities for women to progress professionally as skilled workers, and assume business leadership roles, than their peers in other regions. Gendered power dynamics between spouses, create an additional barrier for women; Recent studies indicate that, women tend to hide their business income from their husbands. As they fear that the husband may end the relationship or reduce their financial contributions to the household. These findings hold for both urban and rural women. Jamaican women are also currently underrepresented in STEM Fields.

The Gender disparity in STEM amongst Jamaican women, extends to disciplines such as computer science, natural sciences, and engineering. According to, the *Planning Institute of Jamaica and the Statistical Institute,* there are a low number of women enrolling, based on the rules. Again, these factors are influenced by gender stereotypes, cultural norms, and lack of access to educational opportunities. More recently, Jamaica has used organizations like the *'Jamaica Computer Society'* and the scientific research council, have launched programs and campaigns to encourage more women and girls to pursue STEM education careers. Similar to the Global #BeMedigitalinclusion inclusion program, these initiatives provide mentoring and networking opportunities and support women's participation in STEM.

Another country is close to my heart because the experience these women have experienced is very similar to my lived experiences. These *'sister leaders'* in this country and are my inspiration! The under-representation of Black women in STEM in the USA–has been a big concern. These women face multiple barriers, such as racial and gender biases, lack of access to resources and opportunities, and social and cultural factors. As a child, growing up in a two-parent household, my parents were very involved in my educational journey. I remember our parents buying a set of children's encyclopaedias that included every piece of information you could think of. Our parents made us read it every single night. My father's love of maths contributed to our early morning timetable rituals. Education was our mantra; by the time we got to primary school, we all could read well and good at maths and the sciences. Something happens, when we get to the classroom, that causes an interruption. One thing I know is this; the foundation is solid from home; even though we experience disruptions, we still rise. Despite having a good foundation, the systematic barriers in place continue to disrupt our journey.

Chapter 9 - Overview: UNITED STATES

Cynthia says she puts this situation down to the *"intersectional leaky pipeline"*; her spin, on the so-called 'leaky pipeline. A metaphor, for the progressive loss of competent women from senior positions, in the fields of science, technology, engineering, and mathematics (STEM).[172]

Education Attainment Gaps

Although, Black women in the US are the most educated group. Disparities, still exist in STEM fields; thankfully, the Covid-19 pandemic, allows us to rectify this. Year after year, we see thousands of unfilled positions in STEM and more than 3 million jobs, estimated in STEM, will need to be filled by 2025. The Pandemic is our chance to fix the Black Women in the STEM Gap[173]. In the US, the struggle to increase diversity in the STEM workforce, especially among Black women, still, persists. The workforce gaps in STEM, relate to pipeline leaks in K-12 and post-secondary education. The perception in high school, fewer women and racial minorities expect to have a career in STEM, at the age of 30. However, in college, significantly more men than women declare STEM majors, and more Asian and white students disclose STEM majors more than their counterparts do. Despite women comprising over half of the workforce, they remain underrepresented in specific high-paying STEM sectors, such as computer and engineering. There were more college degrees earned in 2018 by women (58%) than men. Still, women comprised only 22% of bachelor's degrees in engineering and 19% of bachelor's degrees in computer science[174]. Another critical point to consider regarding educational attainment is the wealth gap. Let's chew on this for a moment; Black women get a good education from home; and they, do much better than their white counterparts. However, these women are being pushed into other careers, paying notably, less than they have achieved educationally. As a result, this is having an impact on Black women's wealth.

Wealth

Workforce: I have heard it all before! Despite all the different incentives and considerable growth in recent years to get more Black and Hispanic workers into the

(STEM) workforce, they are still underrepresented. I have noticed that the widespread representation of STEM occupations for Black women varies largely in health-related jobs, but not in physical Science, computing, engineering, and web3. The Pew Research Center analysis of federal employment and education data, suggests that the current trends in STEM degree attainment, appear unlikely to narrow these gaps substantially[175].

Wealth gaps: Since 2016, there has been no genuine change in STEM jobs. Only 11% of Black workers are employed, and 9% are in STEM occupations. When you break this down further, their share is even lower at 5%; we must look at the long-term representation in STEM education, starting from the early years of schooling to university. They disadvantage Black women from the very beginning. STEM attainment degrees are unlikely to narrow the Tech gaps. Now, most undergraduates earn a degree, yet there's still a disparity in engineering and computer science. In addition to an under-representation of Black women receiving degrees in STEM fields. There is a lack of diversity in STEM, even with all the efforts to accommodate the growth in STEM jobs to reach an all-high and overtake non-STEM positions in the coming years - We have a huge problem! I know the lack of financial resources during early education, school funding, biases in school policies, and lack of economic resources at home. Black women will continue to be displaced if we continue like this.

There's a global concern, but Black women get the worst treatment. You can see that, historically the lack of representation of Black women in STEM in Ghana, Jamaica, and the US has come with deep-rooted and systematic challenges and disparities in the following areas: Wealth, Health, Pay, Mental Health, and Housing. I will make references to all themes below:

Now brace yourself; this is big! The wealth gap is a major problem for Black women in these three countries, affecting their ability to pursue STEM opportunities and access resources. Honestly, it has been too hard to access data, because of the lack of availability. But I have seen other economic indicators, which I will share with you to strengthen my case. In *Ghana*, the World Bank, suggests that the poverty amongst women, is higher than that of men; this shows a wealth gap that impacts on opportunities for women in STEM. In Jamaica, a study conducted by the *'Planning Institute of Jamaica'* showed that women's income levels are lower than men's. Proposing, that a wealth gap could hinder their participation. For the *USA*, the data shows that Black women face wealth disparities compared to other racial and gender groups, influencing their access to quality education and resources in STEM. These three countries show the state of Black women, and it is a genuine concern for me, especially about climate action. If Black women cannot access STEM opportunities, this will mean further exclusion. We know that they give back to their community and if they cannot feed their family, they become depressed. So, what will happen to climate action? I, personally, will be asking Global leaders, to include Black women and fast.

Health

Another significant issue is health disparities, especially around accessibility to healthcare and representation in healthcare professions – which has also significantly impacted the participation of Black women in STEM. In *Ghana*, I have seen that health disparities affect both rural and urban populations, with limited access to quality healthcare facilities and resources for all. This indirect barrier stops Black women accessing and pursuing STEM opportunities in Jamaica, with some women facing higher rates of cervical cancer. Again, this shows disparities in health and indirectly impacts their engagement in STEM fields. In the *USA*, Black women's health disparities, include high maternal mortality rates and higher rates of chronic diseases like hypertension and diabetes. These disparities will harm these Black women pursuing and succeeding in STEM careers.

Pay

The pay gap is another factor contributing to significant differences that these women are experiencing access in all three countries, and Black women are often facing other racial disparities with this pay gap. In *Ghana*, there's not much data on the gender pay gap, especially for African women in STEM; this could be for many reasons; these Ghanaian women are entrepreneurs and look after their families and home. However, the disparities still exist across many industries, indicating the challenges that Black women experience. Again, data on this in *Jamaica* is limited, but according to the statistical institute of Jamaica, women earn lower wages than men in these areas. Again, this is so discouraging to see, and this has been the norm for so many years; just unacceptable. In the *USA*, the data is clear from the U.S. Bureau of Labour Statistics and studies–suggesting that Black women face a pay gap compared with their white and male counterparts, especially in STEM occupations.

Mental Health

Mental health and well-being have been a unique challenge for Black women. Ghana and Jamaica have stigmatized issues around mental health. What's also interesting, is the lack of access to mental healthcare services, especially supporting Black women in

STEM. These factors can contribute to affecting our mental health and contribute to lower retention rates in STEM.

When my father died, right after Covid-19 happened, I suffered from General Anxiety Disorder (GAD); I remembered that my access to support was limited. I could not believe it. I used the famous words from Maya Angelou, if you cannot change something, change your attitude; And so, I did. Furthermore, I am now a better person, having that self-belief.

Working on yourself, and developing a resilient attitude when dealing with life, is essential. I noticed that during Covid-19 period, and getting to the Dr, was a real challenge. But I stopped getting annoyed and just kept trying. However, three years on, I still have not seen my doctor. The NHS system needs fixing! USA studies show that Black women face higher stress levels. This is because of intersectional factors, that can affect our mental health and lower retention in STEM, when considering gaps. In particular, around pay, health, housing, earnings, education attainment, and personal finances, especially for Black women in STEM, which are often limited. However, we must pay attention to the systemic disparities, such as racial biases in housing, wage gaps and educational inequalities, which can indirectly impact Black women's opportunities and success in STEM. The #BeMedigtialinclusion addresses these disparities and has put forward a ten-year strategic plan. I did this plan in 2017 because of the challenges I have experienced and the lack of financial support; it has taken me, nearly five years, to get to this point. Despite this challenge, I will continue to move forward no matter what. To deal with these disparities, I suggest the following:

- Promote educational opportunities and STEM | AI |Web 3 programs targeted and support Black women and girls.

- Implementing policies that address pay equity and ensure fair compensation for Black women and girls in STEM.

- Improving access to quality health care and mental health services with a focus on eliminating racial disparities.

- Collaborating with other organizations to provide affordable housing and create inclusive environments that support Black women in STEM.

- Encouraging financial literacy and providing resources to empower.

Chapter 10 - What is AI?

What is artificial intelligence (AI)? Artificial intelligence is **the simulation of human intelligence processes by machines, especially computer systems**. Specific applications of AI include expert systems, natural language processing, speech recognition, and machine vision.

My reasoning for promoting the #BeMedigitalinclusion program is simply because of my lived experiences. The lack of opportunities for career progression, career advancement, sponsorship, unequal pay and having to deal with racial discrimination. Including, being overlooked for leadership promotion. Even when I got access, I still had to deal with the term they gave me *'Imposter syndrome'*, knowing that I was good. But not seeing Black women in senior leadership roles, made me believe that I was not deserving to be there, and this affected my mental health. The doubt I had for myself was just overwhelming, and I felt less than and undeserving of any success–and this is where imposter syndrome sets in. I'm a Black British woman and don't want our stories to get lost! But with the fast pace of technology. I feel, so many of us, have been disproportionately affected by Covid-19. Having had to deal with job loss, family members dying, our health deteriorating. Notwithstanding, our mental health, and the fact that, the skills we had, were being replaced with digital skills. This gap is widening and the impact of Covid-19, and the issues around diversity and inclusion, are causing us to be left behind. Yet we are talented, gifted, and innovative; we are problem solvers and have creative minds. Now, with an AI tool introduced into the mainstream, I am concerned that if misused, it will reproduce existing racial biases. If Black women are involved with the AI life cycle and understand it, they can live and create a fairer society. Black women must be at every stage of the AI model process. *Suppose the data used to train an AI model captures societal biases?* In that case, this will be present in the recruitment process: healthcare, education, criminal justice, and the AI model will perpetuate those biases, when making predictions or decisions related to Black women.

#BeMedigitalinIcusion AI app

The #BeMedigitalinIcusion AI app addresses these biases by actively improving data collection processes, ensuring diverse representation, and implementing techniques to mitigate biases during model training and evaluation.

In an ideal world, once our Black women have gone through the #BeMedigitalinclusion program, we will have Black women data scientists, Machine Learning experts and developers able to select appropriate algorithms and techniques based on a given problem and available data and be part of creating a solution. This stage will also involve splitting the data into training, validation, and testing the datasets. During the training stages, the AI model learns patterns and relationships in the data. The model is exposed to the training dataset and adjusts its internal parameters iteratively to minimize the difference between its prediction and desired outputs. This process involves running the data through the model multiple times (epochs) to improve accuracy.

Once, training is complete. Validating the AI dataset can be evaluated. Here, we can assess its performance, identify any issues or limitations, and fine-tune the model parameters. At this stage, the validation is critical, especially for ensuring that the model generalizes well- unseen data and performs reliably. Now, the model's performance is tested against real-world scenarios, checking, it continues to meet the desired objectives and addresses any issues that arise. To keep the model and the data relevant, regular updates and retraining are necessary to keep the model up to-date and responsive to changing outcomes.

What I like about the AI model, is that it is, an iterative process. Feedback from users and monitoring data can provide valuable insights for further improvements. This iteration process, allows for continuous refinement and enhancement of the AI software, leading to better performance and user satisfaction. We can create ethical AI software with the right people - it also depends on the organizations, problem domain, and available resources.

The Oppressive Side of AI

The oppressive side of AI sees it spewing, all kinds of biases and I must share with you, what this looks like, so you fully understand the issue at stake here. In the AI stages of development, we see biases introduced at different levels, and societal biases can be present in the training data. If we want to develop an AI model and don't have enough diverse representation, for example, in particular Black women, which will then lead to, under-representation and biases. If the training data consists of white images, then the AI model results will not perform as accurately, when recognizing or classifying images of Black women. The issue for Black women, is that they need to be part of the design process to rid of these unconscious and unrealistic biases. Another societal discrimination is when we present labelling and annotation in the training data. Suppose we have an individual with prejudiced ideas about Black women; the annotations will contain stereotypes and biases, which may lead to model learning and perpetuating these biases.

Based on the current data, there is a lack of Black women in tech - let's assume that the individual who has access to write and create the code is a white man. This man has received instructions to annotate and label the dataset. He may introduce his interpretation of Black women, and the AI model may generate or reinforce discriminatory results.

An example is data collection methods. I referred to this, when advising the UN Pulse on developing an AI ethical framework for Ghana. I shared those biases which arose, because of the methods used to collect training the data. The Ghanaian community needed to be part of this process and not be left out. It also applies to Black women; if the data collection process systematically excludes or overlooks the experiences of Black women, the resulting dataset will be incomplete, unrealistic, and biased, leading to bias AI model. If you have ever attended any of my AI summits or conferences, you would have heard my mantra on the historical biases and discrimination, which plague our society; I reflect on my concerns in the training data.

We must ensure that they include Black women in every process and at every stage. Suppose the data used to train an AI model captures societal biases; this will be present in recruitment employment, healthcare, and the criminal justice system, and the AI model will perpetuate those biases when making predictions or decisions related to Black women.

The #BeMedigitalinclusion AI App addresses these biases by actively improving the data collection process, ensuring diverse representation and implementing techniques to mitigate bias during model training and evaluation.

I will consider some everyday use cases, when AI is presented. Facial recognition tools have the potential to decide, whether you deserve the job or not. HireVue claims it uses artificial intelligence to determine who's best for a job; when I first saw this, I was deeply disturbed by it. It got me thinking about how this AI tool is a gatekeeper for some of the most prominent organizations, reshaping how they assess their workforce and how prospective employees prove their worth.

About five years ago, I started speaking about AI; the name global disruptor came about because I wanted to discuss how oppressive the AI tool could be. Having to deal with this entrepreneurial journey, I recognized the challenges as a founder, which was identical to when I worked in the private and public sectors.

Then I realized that the AI tool could secretly disadvantage Black women further without us even realizing it. I first watched the documentary 'Coded Bias' (2020) by Shalini Kantayya and Dr Buolamwini, which inspired me to start investigating more, about facial recognition tools. I saw the potential barriers for Black women in recruitment. We are already dealing with a daily lack of career advancement, promotion, and racial discrimination. Also, not having any representation of us in the STEM sector and having to deal with the so-called imposter syndrome. I have applied for so many jobs, have been told a big fat no with no honest feedback, and left feeling depleted. However, I always get the unpaid voluntary director | Non-Executive Director roles. Now we have this AI facial recognition tech system, which will select individuals for these positions.

HireVue

This system uses candidates' computer or mobile phone camera to analyse their facial movements, word choice and speaking voice before ranking them against other applicants based on an automatically generated 'employability' score.

My problem here is not with the gatekeeper, but the one creating the algorithmic code, to help decide a person's career. Here are my questions–how does this AI system recruitment tool differentiate between a productive worker and a worker who isn't the right fit? Based on their facial movements, tone of voice, and cultural mannerism? How certain are we, that the individual responsible for this AI development has not included their cultural bias in the system? This process is unfair because this AI is shaping those interviewed.

I noticed this same issue with the live facial recognition tech by the police, where I spoke and presented at *'The Future of Gang and Knife Crime Prevention (2021)'*, on facial recognition tool, hosted by, *The Institute of Government and Public Policy*. I shared how this tool exacerbates racist outcomes in policing, especially in areas like Newham London, which is the most ethnically diverse local authority. As a member of Newham

Independent Advisory Group, I see that, there is a lack of trust within the community. What's more, as a tech community leader at the grassroots level, I've had first-hand experience with gangs and realized, they were so advanced in using tech intelligently. Often, to strategize and have a stronghold, within London and the county lines. I know racial profiling by the police, leads to disproportionate arrests of Black boys, because I have checked the Major for Policing and *'Crime Data Dashboard'* website and seen the police data, shared at these community meetings.

The facial recognition tech uses arrest data (mug shots) borne from discrimination, and this data continues to fuel more racial discrimination via surveillance of the Black community.

AI and the Future

Artificial intelligence (AI) is both omnipresent and, conceptually, slippery. Making it very difficult to regulate. Right now, two major experiments in the design of AI governance, are currently playing out in Europe and China. The European Union (EU) is racing to pass its draft Artificial Intelligence Act - a sweeping piece of legislation, intended to govern nearly all uses of AI. Meanwhile, China is rolling out a series of regulations targeting specific types of algorithms and AI capabilities. Other countries starting their own AI governance initiatives which will learn from the successes and failures of these two, initial efforts to govern AI, will be crucial. The future of Artificial Intelligence (AI) will be a significant contributor to the global economy. However, as AI continues to advance, it presents both opportunities and challenges that require thoughtful consideration and strategic planning.

AI technologies, have the potential to revolutionize various industries, from healthcare and finance to manufacturing and transportation. These innovations can enhance productivity, streamline processes, and drive economic growth. To fully harness the economic potential of AI, it is crucial for the countries to invest in research and development while fostering a vibrant ecosystem of startups and scale-ups.

The digital revolution has brought about a seismic shift in how businesses operate and how consumers interact with products and services. However, this rapid transformation has also exposed a series of key challenges for Black women business owners in the realm of regulation and governance. We must address these challenges to ensure a harmonious integration of digital technologies into our society and economy, including a smooth process for Black women to be included.[176]

Currently, in the UK, there are over ten different regulators having jurisdiction over various aspects of digital technologies, there's often overlap and contradiction in mandates. The fragmentation of regulation creates confusion for businesses and for Black women SMEs, as they try to navigate a complex web of regulatory requirements. I welcome the Digital Regulation Co-operation Forum, which is a step in the right direction. The aim is to streamline regulatory processes and foster cooperation among regulators. Moving forward, a more cohesive regulatory landscape is essential, to providing clarity and reduce compliance burdens, which Black women face daily.

We can see how technology is going at lightning speed, and this is delaying regulatory systems to respond effectively, which is having an impact on Black women. To strike the right balance, regulatory agencies must adopt agile approaches that allow for experimentation, adaptation, and swift responses to emerging technologies. Establishing mechanisms for ongoing dialogue between Black women, the industry, and regulators who can help to facilitate this balance. Ensuring that regulations develop alongside technology. This will be a win for us all.

The big challenge is the skills gap in AI, data analytics, and responsible data governance, to address and move forward. Investments should be made in the Global #BeMedigitalinclusion training and capacity building program, for Black women in collaboration with regulators. This will help to bridge the digital skills gap and ensure that regulators have the right knowledge and expertise needed to understand and oversee advanced technologies effectively, concurrently allowing Black women to be part of this development process.

To address these key challenges in digital AI regulation is essential for fostering innovation, ensuring public trust, and harnessing the full potential of digital technologies for economic growth and societal benefit. A collaborative and adaptive approach involving government, regulators, industry, and academia is vital to navigate the evolving digital landscape successfully.

Round Up

We must include Black women in AI and machine learning. This is important for the future because their involvement, promises to enrich the development of advanced technologies. Their unique perspectives, experiences, and insights are invaluable assets in shaping the future of AI. As entities like OpenAI and technologies like ChatGPT continue to rise, the urgency to address the challenges associated with AI becomes increasingly apparent. The growing proliferation of AI and data-driven solutions amplifies the need for greater diversity in the creation of these technologies. Black women, often underrepresented in tech, will bring a wealth of diverse viewpoints that can enhance the ethical considerations, fairness, and real-world applicability of AI systems. Their participation can help mitigate unconscious, unrealistic biases, ensure equitable outcomes, and foster innovation that benefits all the society. To harness the full potential of AI, we must actively promote diversity and inclusion in AI research, development, and decision-making processes, recognizing that the strength of AI lies in its ability to reflect and serve the diversity of the world it affects.

In response to pro-innovation Regulation of Technologies review, when including Black women's involvement in drones, data, space, and satellite technologies, and cybersecurity, the government must enact strategic reforms to stimulate economic growth and innovation. While addressing regulatory challenges and promoting industry expansion, it is imperative to emphasize diversity and inclusion. Black women, when actively included, bring unique perspectives that enrich these sectors, fostering equitable and ethical advancements. By embracing their contributions, we can ensure that emerging technologies, benefit society while avoiding biases and inequalities, shaping a future that is both innovative and inclusive.

Paulette Watson

She, Disrupts!

Awards

Winner

UK:

2023 - The 50 Most Influential women in the U.K. Technology
2023 - 2023- Women in Tech Excellence
2023- Computing IT Leader 100
2023- Inspirational Businesswomen in STEM & Construction
2022- KPMG Black Entrepreneur's awards 2022
2019- Red Bull Amaphiko mentoring Award UK 2019

Global awards

2023- Women changing World Awards | SILVER for the category Entrepreneur of the Year
2023- Global Caribbean Awards Best Innovator and Caribbean Excellence
2022- Top 100 Women of the Future: Metaverse and Web 3
2021- Most Skilful Shepreneur for the Ghana Ladies in Tech (GLiT)
2019- Wintrade Global Award Women in Engineering

Nominations: 2023
2023 - Baton Awards.
2023- CRN Women & Diversity in Channel Awards
2023- The Women's Business Awards
2023- The Social Mobility Project Awards for The Inclusive Awards
2022- We are Tech Women 100 Global Award for Achievement

Finalist:

2023- UK IT Industry Awards (BCS Computing)
2023- Entrepreneur of the Year Award at the Black Tech Achievement Awards
2023- Women in IT–Social Impact of the Year 2023
2022- Black Tech Achievement Awards–Entrepreneur
2021- Women in Tech Excellence Awards
2021- BLAC Awards Community Entrepreneur
2021- National Diversity Awards-Community Age–Finalist
2022- Long list for the 2022 Rising Women in Crypto Power List, October 2022

Recognised for: Tech Women 50 Celebration showcases the women making waves in all sorts of areas of tech right now.

REFERENCES

[1] Gjersoe, Nathalia, *Bridging the gender gap: why do so few girls study stem subjects* The Guardian. https://www.theguardian.com/science/head-quarters/2018/mar/08/bridging-the-gender-gap-why-do-so-few-girls-study-stem-subjects. Accessed 9 June 2020.

[2] Ditto

[3] Women in STEM Week 2021: *How we're empowering the next generation, accessed 30 June 2021.* https://educationhub.blog.gov.uk/2021/02/11/women-in-stem-week-2021-how-were-empowering-the-next-generation/

[4] *Record numbers of women in STEM*, says report from FE News- https://aspiretohe.co.uk/news_article/record-numbers-of-women-in-stem-says-report/. Accessed 23rd November 2021. And Women in STEM Week 2021: *How we're empowering the next generation, June 2021*)

[5] Women in STEM Week 2021: *How we're empowering the next generation, accessed 30 June 2021.* https://educationhub.blog.gov.uk/2021/02/11/women-in-stem-week-2021-how-were-empowering-the-next-generation/

[6] Evening Standard, *Tech under fire for failure to hire Black employees*, 22 Nov 2019. https://www.standard.co.uk/business/tech-under-fire-for-failure-to-hire-Black-employees-a4293836.html

[7] Tech Nation, *What % of People Working in Tech are from BAME Background?* 22 Aug 2018. https://technation.io/news/what-of-people-working-in-tech-are-from-bame-backgrounds/

[8] Dame Alison Marie Rose-Slade DBE is a British banker, who was chief executive (CEO) of NatWest Group from November 2019 to July 2023

[9] British Computer Society (BCS), The Chartered Institute for IT, *The Experiences of Black Women in The Information Technology Industry*. October 2022.

[10] UK Government, The changing face of business: number of women on FTSE boards up by 50% in just 5 years - GOV.UK (www.gov.uk). February 2021

[11] Population of England and Wales 22 December 2022. — https://www.ethnicity-facts-figures.service.gov.uk/uk-population-by-ethnicity/national-and-regional-populations/population-of-england-and-wales/latest

[12] The Health Foundation: *Black and Minority Ethnic workers make up a disproportionately large share of key worker sectors in London* - https://www.health.org.uk/Black-and-minority-ethnic-workers-make-up-a-disproportionately-large-share-of-key-worker-sectors-in

[13] The McGregor-Smith Review, *Race in the Workplace*. https://www.gov.uk/government/publications/race-in-the-workplace-the-mcgregor-smith-review

[14] BBSTEM University Alliance, https://bbstem.co.uk/bbstem-uni-alliance/

[15] ONS, *BCS Diversity Report 2020: ONS Analysis Part 2 / 2* BCS, The Chartered Institute for IT, 24 June 2020

[16] BCS – The Chartered Institute for IT, *Record Number of Women in IT, but Black Women are Still Underrepresented,* 23 Sept 2020. https://www.bcs.org/more/about-us/press-office/press-releases/record-numbers-of-women-in-it-but-Black-women-still-under-represented-new-research-finds/

[17] Computer Weekly – More *than 20% of tech employees hesitant to speak about diversity.* Accessed 5th March 2021

[18] Sic

[19] Data Science and Cybersecurity - Thousands *of Black women 'missing' from the IT industry.* 27th October 2022 - https://www.bcs.org/articles-opinion-and-research/thousands-of-Black-women-missing-from-the-it-industry-report-warns/

[20] BCS, *Record Numbers of Women in IT but Black Women Still Under-Represented* | https://www.bcs.org/more/about-us/press-office/press-releases/record-numbers-of-women-in-it-but-Black-women-still-under-represented-new-research-finds/

[21] UNESCO, *gender imbalances remain in digital skills and STEM careers.* 1st May 2023 -https://uis.unesco.org/en/blog/gender-imbalances-remain-digital-skills-stm-careers

[22] UNESCO. *Women in Science.* Fs51-women-in-science-2018-en.pdf (unesco.org)

[23] UNESCO. *Science Report Towards 2030.* Published in 2015 by the United Nations Educational, Scientific and Cultural Organization https://uis.unesco.org/sites/default/files/documents/unesco-science-report-towards-2030-part1.pdf. Accessed 7th June 2020

[24] Priner, Katrina. *Portugal ranked a top country for women in Tech.* https://southeusummit.com/europe/portugal/portugal-ranked-top-country-women-tech/, South EU Summit. Accessed 3rd March 2020.

[25] Asere Anda, *Proportional of women in IT in Latvia ranges from 20 to 29%* - https://labsoflatvia.com/en/news/proportion-of-women-in-it-in-latvia-ranges-from-20-to-29. Labs of Latvia. March 2023.

[26] Population of England and Wales, published 22nd December 2022

[27] Commons Library, Parliament. https://commonslibrary.parliament.uk/research-briefings/cbp-9023/ Accessed 21st August 2021

[28] Publications, Parliament. Accessed 16th June 2023; https://publications.parliament.uk/pa/cm5803/cmselect/cmsctech/95/report.html#footnote-222

[29] Stem Education Journal. https://stemeducationjournal.springeropen.com/articles/10.1186/s40594-018-0115-6

[30] Tech London Advocates. https://www.techlondonadvocates.org.uk/The-London-Tech-Manifesto-2021.pdf

[31] Wise Campaign. Accessed October 2021 https://www.wisecampaign.org.uk/women-in-stem-workforce-2017/

[32] Tech Crunch. Accessed October 2021 https://techcrunch.com/2016/05/10/the-lack-of-women-in-tech-is-more-than-a-pipeline-problem/

[33] Tech Crunch. Accessed October 2021. https://techcrunch.com/2016/05/10/the-lack-of-women-in-tech-is-more-than-a-pipeline-problem/

[34] PWC Davros Programme. https://www.pwc.com/gx/en/about/contribution-to-debate/world-economic-forum/pwc-at-davos.html Accessed October 2021

[35] BBC News. Accessed October 2021 https://www.bbc.co.uk/news/education-31733742

[36] AND Digital. *The Nature of the Digital Gap.* https://landing.and.digital/uk_digital_skills_gap

[37] Virgin Media O2 Business. *Virgin Media 02 Business Launches National Public Sector...*https://news.virginmediao2.co.uk/virgin-media-o2-business-launches-national-public-sector-partnership-programme-to-tackle-the-digital-divide-as-research-finds-five-million-brits-unable-to-carry-out-simple-tasks-online/ Accessed November 2022

[38] Assets. Publishing Service. UK Government. https://assets.publishing.service.gov.uk/government/uploads/system/uploads/attachment_data/file/686071/Revised_RDA_report_March_2018.pdf

[39] Geragthy, Liam., The Big Issue. *Twice as many women as men are living in London's temporary accommodation.* March 2022. https://www.bigissue.com/news/housing/twice-the-number-of-women-than-men-in-living-in-london-temporary-accommodation/ cited April 2022

[40] STEM Education Journal. Springer Open. https://stemeducationjournal.springeropen.com/articles/10.1186/s40594-018-0115-6

[41] History-Computer. *Asimov Laws of Robotics.* ISBN 978-0-385-09041-4. Accessed 1st August 2022 https://history-computer.com/asimovs-laws-of-robotics/

[42] Ditto

[43] Berkeley School of Information. *How Artificial Intelligence Bias Affects Women of Colour.* https://ischoolonline.berkeley.edu/blog/artificial-intelligence-bias/ cited December 2021

[44] Turner-Lee, Nicol., Resnick, Paul., Barton, Genie., *Algorithmic Bias Detection and Migration: best practices and policies to reduce consumer harms.* https://www.brookings.edu/articles/algorithmic-bias-detection-and-mitigation-best-practices-and-policies-to-reduce-consumer-harms/ cited December 2021

[45] van der Meulen, Rob., McCall, Thomas., *Gartner Says Nearly Half of CIOs Are Planning to Deploy Artificial Intelligence.* February 2018. https://www.gartner.com/en/newsroom/press-releases/2018-02-13-gartner-says-nearly-half-of-cios-are-planning-to-deploy-artificial-intelligence. Cited January 2022

[46] Washington Post. Accessed 22nd January 2022.
https://www.washingtonpost.com/technology/2021/12/02/timnit-gebru-dair/

[47] Highlighted at The Future of Gang and knife Crime Prevention 2021- Institute of Government & Public Policy: Paulette Watson presentation on Digital policing tools.

[48] Lau, Tim., *Predictive Policing Explained*. April 2020.
https://www.brennancenter.org/our-work/research-reports/predictive-policing-explained, cited April 2022

[49] Bush, Vannevar., *The Endless Frontier*. National Science Foundation: where discoveries begin. United States Government Printing Office, Washington. 1945. Accessed 1st May 2022.
https://www.nsf.gov/about/history/nsf50/vbush1945_content.jsp

[50] Rothwell, Jonathan., *The Hidden Stem Economy*. Metropolitan Policy Programme. Brookings. 2013. Accessed 1st May 2022.
https://www.brookings.edu/wp-content/uploads/2016/06/TheHiddenSTEMEconomy610.pdf

[51] World Economic Forum. *The Future of Jobs 2018*. 17th September 2018.
https://www.weforum.org/reports/the-future-of-jobs-report-2018/

[52] Heinrich, Sen. Martin. Joint Economic Committee, Democrats. *Ten Ways Stem Strengthens The Economy*. jec.senate.gov.
https://www.jec.senate.gov/public/_cache/files/2061de0c-be23-4cf1-ad0b-270d3f6c661e/stem-top-10-12.4-final-1-pager.pdf

[53] Deming, David J. and Noray, Kadeem L., *Stem Careers And The Changing Skill Requirements Of Work*, Working Paper 25065, Nber Working Paper Series, National Bureau Of Economic Research. Revised June 2019.
https://www.nber.org/system/files/working_papers/w25065/w25065.pdf

[54] Heinrich, U.S. Senator Martin., *Ten Ways STEM Strengths The Economy*, Joint Economic Committee Democrats, jec.senate.gov. Accessed 1st September 2022.

[55] Hogan, Andrew and Roberts, Brian., *Occupational Employment Projections to 2024*, Monthly Labour Review. December 2015. Accessed 1st September 2022.
https://www.bls.gov/opub/mlr/2015/article/occupational-employment-projections-to-2024.htm

[56] Assets. Publishing Service. UK Government. Accessed 22nd October 2021
https://assets.publishing.service.gov.uk/government/uploads/system/uploads/attachment_data/file/461479/BIS-15-544-digital-health-in-the-uk-an-industry-study-for-the-Office-of-Life-Sciences.pdf

[57] Standing, Mike., and Hampson, Elizabeth., *Digital Health in the UK: An industry study for the Office of Life Sciences*, Monitor Deloitte, Office for Life Sciences. September 2015. Accessed 6th May 2022.
https://assets.publishing.service.gov.uk/government/uploads/system/uploads/attachment_data/file/461479/BIS-15-544-digital-health-in-the-uk-an-industry-study-for-the-Office-of-Life-Sciences.pdf

[58] KPMG, *Exploring Gender Inequity in the Context of COVID-19: Investing With a Gender Lens*. Notes from a panel session presentation at the Gender Lens Investment Summit 2021 in Pyrmont, New South Wales, Australia on 18th May 2021. https://home.kpmg/xx/en/home/insights/2021/06/gender-lens-investing.html

[59] Google, *We're Growing To Meet People Where They Are*, 2022 Diversity Annual Report. Accessed 1st September 2022. https://about.google/belonging/diversity-annual-report/2022/

[60] Standing, Mike., and Hampson, Elizabeth., *Digital Health in the UK: An industry study for the Office of Life Sciences*, Monitor Deloitte, Office for Life Sciences. September 2015. Accessed 1st September 2022. https://assets.publishing.service.gov.uk/government/uploads/system/uploads/attachment_data/file/461479/BIS-15-544-digital-health-in-the-uk-an-industry-study-for-the-Office-of-Life-Sciences.pdf

[61] Durman, Andy., *Focus On The Demand For Stem Jobs & Skills In Britain*, Emsi. Accessed 1st September 2022. https://www.economicmodelling.co.uk/wp-content/uploads/2018/12/STEM-Report_vWEB.pdf

[62] Camden, Billy., *Black Girls Take The Lead in STEM Subjects*. Schools Week. October 2023. **https://schoolsweek.co.uk/Black-girls-take-the-lead-in-stem-subjects/.**

[63] Publications. Parliament. Accessed April 2023 https://publications.parliament.uk/pa/cm5803/cmselect/cmsctech/95/report.html

[64] Commons Library. Parliament. Accessed April 2023. https://commonslibrary.parliament.uk/research-briefings/cbp-9195/

[65] Bulman, Hayri., *The Increasing Demand for STEM Subjects Skills*, Britain News Time. Accessed 1st September 2022. https://britainnewstime.com/2022/09/16/the-increasing-demand-for-stem-subjects-skills/

[66] Yahoo. tbps://uk.sports.yahoo.com/news/stem-skills-shortage-costing-uk-businesses-1-5Bn-report-says-093608643.html. Accessed January 2022

[67] ditto

[68] Gulliver, Kevin., *Racial Discrimination in UK Housing has a Long History and Deep Roots*, December 2017. https://eprints.lse.ac.uk/85294/1/politicsandpolicy-racial-discrimination-in.pdf. Accessed 1st September 2022.

[69] Constellation. https://www.constellation.com/energy-101/what-is-a-smart-home.html. Accessed 1st September 2022

[70] Chan, M.; Campo, E.; Estève, D.; Fourniols, J.Y. *Smart homes—current features and future perspectives*. Maturitas 2009, 64, 90–97. [Cross Ref]

[71] Paetz, A.G.; Dütschke, E.; Fichtner, W. *Smart homes as a means to sustainable energy consumption: A study of consumer perceptions*. J. Consum. Policy 2012,35, 23–41. [Cross Ref]

[72] Solar for America, *Take Back Control of Your Energy*, Accessed 5th May 2022. https://solar4america.org/solar

[73] Gartner, John., *Meet George Jetson's House*. Wired Staff. January 2000 https://www.wired.com/2000/01/meet-george-jetsons-house/. Cited October 2022

[74] Smith, Micha-Shannon., and Luminate, Prospects, *In The UK Stem's Skill Shortage* by, Jun 2020. Accessed 14th July 2021

[75] Perry, Tristan., *Why Are Smart Homes "Bad"? 19 Disadvantages To Consider*, Smart Home Point. February 2020. Accessed 5th May 2022. https://www.smarthomepoint.com/disadvantages/

[76] International Atomic Energy Agency: *Climate Change and Nuclear Power*, 2020. Accessed January 2021. https://www-pub.iaea.org/MTCD/Publications/PDF/PUB1911_web.pdf

[77] Barath Raghavan and Justin Ma. *The Energy and Emergy of the Internet*. Accessed January 2022 https://www1.icsi.berkeley.edu/pubs/networking/energyandemergy11.pdf

[78] Venkatesh, V.; Davis, F.D. *A theoretical extension of the technology acceptance model: Four longitudinal field studies*. Manag. Sci. 2000,46, 186–204. [Cross Ref]

[79] Venkatesh, V.; Morris, M.G.; Davis, G.B.; Davis, F.D. *User acceptance of inform ation technology: Toward an unified view*. MIS Q. 2003, 425–478. [Cross Ref]

[80] Brown, Susan A., Venkatesh, Viswanath., and Hoehle, Hartmut, *Technology Adoption Decisions in the Household: a Seven-model Comparison*, ASSIST. December 2014. https://asistdl.onlinelibrary.wiley.com/doi/epdf/10.1002/asi.23305

[81] Kim, H.W.; Chan, H.C.; Gupta, S. *Value-based adoption of mobile internet: An empirical investigation*. Decis. Support Syst. 2007, 43, 111–126. [Cross Ref]

[82] Brush, A.B.; Lee, B.; Mahajan, R.; Agarwal, S.; Saroiu, S.; Dixon, C. *Home automation in the wild: Challenges and opportunities*. In Proceedings of the SIGCHI Conference on Human Factors in Computing Systems, Vancouver, BC, Canada, 7–12 May 2011; ACM Press: New York, NY, USA, 2011; pp. 2115–2124. [Cross Ref]

[83] Wilson, C.; Hargreaves, T.; Hauxwell-Baldwin, R. *Smart homes and their users: A systematic analysis and key challenges*. Pers. Ubiquitous Comput. 2015,19, 463–476. [Cross Ref]

[84] Chang, Soojung and Nam, Kyeongsook, *Smart Home Adoption: The Impact of User Characteristics and Differences in Perception of Benefits*, MDPI. 10th July 2021. https://www.mdpi.com/2075-5309/11/9/393/htm. Accessed 1st September 2022.

[85] Davis, F.D.; Bagozzi, R.P.; Warshaw, P.R. *Extrinsic and intrinsic motivation to use computers in the workplace*. J. Appl. Soc. Psychol. 1992,22, 1111–1132. [Cross Ref]

[86] Lin, T.C.; Wu, S.; Hsu, J.S.C.; Chou, Y.C. *The integration of value-based adoption and expectation–confirmation models: An example of IPTV continuance intention*. Decis. Support Syst. 2012,54, 63–75. [Cross Ref]

[87] Kim, Y.; Park, Y.; Choi, J. *A study on the adoption of IoT smart home service: Using Value-based Adoption Model*. Total. Qual. Manag. Bus. Excell. 2017,28, 1149–1165. [Cross Ref]

[88] Davis, F.D. *Perceived usefulness, perceived ease of use, and user acceptance of information technology*. MIS Q. 1989, 13, 319–340. [Cross Ref]

[89] Wu, G. *The mediating role of perceived interactivity in the effect of actual interactivity on attitude toward the website*. J. Interact. Advert. 2005,5, 29–39. [Cross Ref]

[90] Hsu, C.L.; Lin, J.C.C. *Acceptance of blog usage: The roles of technology acceptance, social influence and knowledge sharing motivation*. Inf. Manag. 2008,45, 65–74. [CrossRef]

[91] Van Dijk, J.A.; Peters, O.; Ebbers, W. *Explaining the acceptance and use of government Internet services: A multivariate analysis of 2006 survey data in the Netherlands*. Gov. Inf. Q. 2008,25, 379–399. [CrossRef]

[92] Kim, Y.; Park, Y.; Choi, J. *A study on the adoption of IoT smart home service: Using Value-based Adoption Model*. Total. Qual. Manag. Bus. Excell. 2017,28, 1149–1165. [CrossRef]

[93] Aldossari, M.Q.; Sidorova, A. *Consumer acceptance of Internet of Things (IoT): Smart home context*. J. Comput. Inf. Syst. 2020, 60, 507–517. [CrossRef]

[94] Parag, Y.; Butbul, G. Flexiwatts and seamless technology: Public perceptions of demand flexibility through smart home technology. Energy Res. Soc. Sci. 2018,39, 177–191. [CrossRef]

[95] Luor, T.T.; Lu, H.P.; Yu, H.; Lu, Y. *Exploring the critical quality attributes and models of smart homes*. Maturitas 2015, 82, 377–386. [CrossRef]

[96] ditto

[97] Mennicken, S.; Vermeulen, J. Huang, E.M. *From today's augmented houses to tomorrow's smart homes: New directions for home automation research*. In Proceedings of the 2014 ACM International Joint Conference on Pervasive and Ubiquitous Computing, Washington, DC, USA, 13–17 September 2014; pp. 105–115. [CrossRef]

[98] Noh, M.J.; Kim, J.S. *Factors influencing the user acceptance of digital home services*. Telecommun. Policy, 2010, 34, 672–682. [CrossRef]

[99] Shin, J.; Park, Y.; Lee, D. *Who will be smart home users? An analysis of adoption and diffusion of smart homes*. Technol. Forecast. Soc. Chang. 2018,134, 246–253. [CrossRef]

[100] Luor, T.T.; Lu, H.P.; Yu, H.; Lu, Y. *Exploring the critical quality attributes and models of smart homes*. Maturitas 2015, 82, 377–386. [CrossRef]

[101] Eggen, B.; Hollemans, G.; van de Sluis, R. Exploring and enhancing the home experience. Cogn. Technol. Work. 2003, 5, 44–54. [CrossRef]

[102] Courtney, K.L.; Demeris, G.; Rantz, M.; Skubic, M. *Needing smart home technologies: The perspectives of older adults in continuing care retirement communities*. Inform. Prim. Care 2008,16, 195–201. [CrossRef] [PubMed]

[103] Demiris, G.; Rantz, M.J.; Aud, M.A.; Marek, K.D.; Tyrer, H.W.; Skubic, M.; Hussam, A.A. *Older adults' attitudes towards and perceptions of 'smart home' technologies*: A pilot study. Med. Inform. Internet Med. 2004,29, 87–94. [CrossRef] [PubMed]

[104] Pal, D.; Funilkul, S.; Vanijja, V.; Papasratorn, B. *Analyzing the elderly users' adoption of smart-home services*. IEEE Access 2018,6, 51238–51252. [CrossRef]

[105] Yang, H.; Lee, H.; Zo, H. *User acceptance of smart home services: An extension of the theory of planned behaviour*. Ind. Manag. Data Syst. 2017,117, 68–89. [CrossRef]

[106] Yang, H.; Lee, H.; Zo, H. *User acceptance of smart home services: An extension of the theory of planned behaviour*. Ind. Manag. Data Syst. 2017,117, 68–89. [CrossRef]

[107] Shih, T.-Y. (2013), "Determinates of consumer adoption attitudes: an empirical study of smart home services", International Journal of E-Adoption, Vol. 5 No. 2, pp. 40-56. **Sourced:**
Marco Hubert, Markus Blut, Christian Brock, Ruby Wenjiao Zhang, Vincent Koch, René Riedl. *The influence of acceptance and adoption drivers on smart home usage*.
https://www.emerald.com/insight/content/doi/10.1108/EJM-12-2016-0794/full/html. October 2022

[108] Shin, J.; Park, Y.; Lee, D. *Who will be smart home users? An analysis of adoption and diffusion of smart homes*. Technol. Forecast. Soc. Chang. 2018,134, 246–253. [CrossRef]

[109] Nikou, S. *Factors driving the adoption of smart home technology: An empirical assessment*. Telemat. Inform. 2019, 45, 101283. [CrossRef]

[110] ditto

[111] Balta-Ozkan, N.; Amerighi, O.; Boteler, B. *A comparison of consumer perceptions towards smart homes in the UK, Germany and Italy: Reflections for policy and future research*. Technol. Anal. Strateg. Manag. 2014,26, 1176–1195. [CrossRef]

[112] Williams, T.; Bernold, L.; Lu, H. *Adoption patterns of advanced information technologies in the construction industries of the United States and Korea*. J. Constr. Eng. Manag. 2007,133, 780–790. [CrossRef]

[113] Brush, A.B.; Lee, B.; Mahajan, R.; Agarwal, S.; Saroiu, S.; Dixon, C. *Home automation in the wild: Challenges and opportunities*. In Proceedings of the SIGCHI Conference on Human Factors in Computing Systems, Vancouver, BC, Canada, 7–12 May 2011; ACM Press: New York, NY, USA, 2011; pp. 2115–2124. [CrossRef]

[114] Kim, Junyoung., Lee, Sunwoo., Chun, Sanghee., Han, Areum., Heo, Jinmoo. *The effects of leisure-time physical activity on optimism, life satisfaction, psychological well-being, and positive affect among older adults with loneliness.* Pages 406-415 | Received 26 Sep 2015, Accepted 01 Sep 2016, published online: 03 Oct 2016.

https://www.tandfonline.com/doi/abs/10.1080/11745398.2016.1238308 Cited October 2022

[115] Kim, Y.; Park, Y.; Choi, J. *A study on the adoption of IoT smart home service: Using Value-based Adoption Model*. Total. Qual. Manag. Bus. Excell. 2017,28, 1149–1165. [CrossRef]

[116] Zhenshan, Yang., Cai, Jianming, Qi, Wei. Lu, Shenghe., Deng, Yu, *The Influence of Income, Lifestyle, and Green Spaces on Interregional Migration: Policy Implications for China*. Wiley Online. November 2015. https://onlinelibrary.wiley.com/doi/abs/10.1002/psp.1996 cited October 2022

[117] Yang, H.; Lee, H.; Zo, H. *User acceptance of smart home services: An extension of the theory of planned behaviour*. Ind. Manag. Data Syst. 2017,117, 68–89. [CrossRef]

[118] Shin, Jungwoo., Park, Yuri, Lee, Daeho., *Who will be smart home users? An analysis of adoption and diffusion of smart homes*. Technological Forecasting and Social Change. Volume 134, September 2018, Pages 246-253. Author links open overlay panel. https://www.sciencedirect.com/science/article/abs/pii/S0040162518300696. Cited October 2022

[119] Noh, M.J.; Kim, J.S. *Factors influencing the user acceptance of digital home services*. Telecommun. Policy, 2010, 34, 672–682. [CrossRef]

[120] Yang, H.; Lee, W.; Lee, H. *IoT smart home adoption: The importance of proper level automation*. J. Sens. 2018. [CrossRef]

[121] Venkatesh, V.; Davis, F.D. A theoretical extension of the technology acceptance model: Four longitudinal field studies. Manag. Sci. 2000,46, 186–204. [CrossRef]

[122] Venkatesh, V.; Morris, M.G.; Davis, G.B.; Davis, F.D. *User acceptance of information technology: Toward an unified view*. MIS Q. 2003, 425–478. [CrossRef]

[123] Mamat, M.; Haron, M.S.; Razak, N.S.A. *Personal interaction encounter, customer involvement, familiarity, and customer service experience in Malaysian public universities*. Procedia Soc. Behav. Sci. 2014,130, 293–298. [CrossRef]

[124] Shih, Chuan-Fong, Venkatesh, Alladi., *Beyond Adoption: Development and Application of a Use-Diffusion Model*. Vol 68, Issue 1. January 2004. https://journals.sagepub.com/doi/abs/10.1509/jmkg.68.1.59.24029. Cited October 2022

[125] Shih, C.F.; Venkatesh, A. *Beyond adoption: Development and application of a use-diffusion model*. J. Mark.2004,68, 59–72. [CrossRef]

[126] Nikou, S. *Factors driving the adoption of smart home technology: An empirical assessment*. Telemat. Inform. 2019, 45, 101283. [CrossRef]

[127] Yang, H.; Lee, W.; Lee, H. *IoT smart home adoption: The importance of proper level automation*. J. Sens. 2018. [CrossRef]

[128] Lindsey, Rebecca and Dahlman, Luann., *Climate Change: Global Temperature*. Climate, Gov. https://www.climate.gov/news-features/understanding-climate/climate-change-global-temperature

[129] National Centres for Environmental Information. Annual 2022 Global Climate Report: Monthly Report. https://www.ncei.noaa.gov/access/monitoring/monthly-report/global/202213#:~:text=Despite%20the%20last%20two%20years,0.32°F Accessed January 2022

[130] Lindsey, Rebecca and Dahlman, Luann., *Climate Change: Global Temperature. Climate, Gov.* https://www.climate.gov/news-features/understanding-climate/climate-change-global-temperature

[131] American Journal of Science and Arts, 1986

[132] State of the Planet, *Why Climate Science Needs More Women Scientists*, https://news.climate.columbia.edu/2022/02/11/why-climate-science-needs-more-women-scientists/

[133] Institute for Statistics, *Women In Science*, UNESCO, http://uis.unesco.org/en/topic/women-science, printed 2nd March 2022

[134] Qaisar, Farah., *A New Comprehensive Report Shows How Women in STEM Face Huge Disadvantages*, Massive Science, https://massivesci.com/articles/lancet-women-stem-inequality-sex-discrimination/, printed 2nd March 2022

[135] Moss-Racusin, Corinne. A., Dovidio, John. F., Brescoll, Victoria. L., *Science faculty's subtle gender biases favour male students.* https://www.pnas.org/doi/10.1073/pnas.1211286109. PNAS. September 2012.

[136] Naaz Fathima, Farah., Awor, Phyllis., Yen, Yi-Chun., Angeline Gnanaselvam, Nancy., Zakham, Fathiah, *Challenges and coping strategies faced by female scientists*, PLOS One, Sept 2020 https://journals.plos.org/plosone/article?id=10.1371/journal.pone.0238635#pone.0238635.ref008 . Printed 2nd March 2022

[137] Myers, Kyle R., Tham, Wei Yang., Yin, Yian., Cochodes, Nina., Thursby, Jerry G., Thursby, Marie C., Schiffer., Walsh, Joseph T., Lakhani, Karim R. & Wang, Dashun, *Unequal effects of the COVID-19 pandemic on scientists*, July 2020. https://www.nature.com/articles/s41562-020-0921-y. Printed 2nd March 2022

[138] Reuters. *The Hot List*, explore the @Reuters Hot List of 1,000 top climate scientists. April 2020.

[139] Tandon, Ayesha., *Analysis: the lack of diversity in climate science research*. https://www.carbonbrief.org/analysis-the-lack-of-diversity-in-climate-science-research. October 2021

[140] IUCN. *Gender and climate change*, Gender and climate change | IUCN, Issues Brief

[141] Food and Agriculture Organization of the United Nations. *Why is gender equality and rural women's empowerment central to the work of FAO?* https://www.fao.org/gender/background/en/. Printed 16th April 2022

[142] Mourdoukoutas, Eleni., Women *grapple with harsh weather*. African Youth and Climate Crisis. https://www.un.org/africarenewal/magazine/august-2016/women-grapple-harsh-weather. August – November 2016. Accessed 16th April 2022

[143] Cho, Renee., *Why Climate Science Needs More Women Scientists*, Columbia Climate School Lamont-Doherty Earth Observatory. Why Climate Science Needs More Women Scientists | Lamont-Doherty Earth Observatory (columbia.edu). February 2022.

[144] Study International. *Top STEM degrees in the US to make a difference*. Partner Content. https://www.bbc.com/storyworks/future/the-next-wave-empowering-global-change/women-in-stem. February 2022

[145] Stoet, G., Geary, D.C., *The Gender-Equality Paradox in Science, Technology, Engineering, and Mathematics Education*. Psychological Science. 2018. https://journals.sagepub.com/doi/abs/10.1177/0956797617741719

[146] UNESCO. *UNESCO science report: towards 2030*. UNESCO Science Report: Towards 2030 – WISAT. UNESCO. Accessed 18th April 2022

[147] British Council. *British Council scholarships for women in STEM*. British Council. Accessed 18th April 2022

[148] European Institute for Gender Equality. *How gender equality in STEM education leads to economic growth*. Study Section. How gender equality in STEM education leads to economic growth | EIGE (europa.eu) Accessed 18th April 2022

[149] UNESCO. *UNESCO science report: towards 2030*. UNESCO Science Report: Towards 2030 – WISAT. UNESCO. Accessed 18th April 2022

[150] George, A., *nurses, Community Health, and Home Carers: gendered human resources compensating for skewed health systems*. Global Public Health, April 2008 - Taylor & Francis https://www.tandfonline.com/doi/abs/10.1080/17441690801892240

[151] Sachetti, Florencia Caro and Petrone, Luciana, *Gender Main streaming in the COVID-19 Policy Response Fostering Equality during the Pandemic and Beyond*, CIPPEC. https://www.cippec.org/wp-content/uploads/2021/05/Global-Solutions-Journal-7-Caro-Sachetti-Petrone.pdf Accessed 15th September 2022

[152] Lina Ya'qoub, an Islam Y. Elgendy, b and Carl J. Pepinec. *Sex and gender differences in COVID-19: More to be learned*. Am Heart J Plus. March 2021. Sex and gender differences in COVID-19: More to be learned! - PMC (nih.gov)

[153] WHO Team. *The gender pay gap in the health and care sector, a global analysis in the time of COVID-19*. July 2022. The gender pay gap in the health and care sector, a global analysis in the time of COVID-19 (who.int)

[154] Singh, Kavita and Bloom, Shelah, *Influence of Women's Empowerment on Maternal Health and Maternal Health Care Utilization: A Regional Look at Africa*, https://paa2011.princeton.edu/papers/110362 Accessed 7th August 2022

[155] Verma, Ravi and Srinivasan, Padmavathi., *Theory of Change*, International Center for Research on Women (ICRW). 2014. https://www.icrw.org/publications/theory-of-change-ending-child-marriage-in-bangladesh/. Accessed 4th September 2022

[156] UN Women, UNDP and the Pardee, S. Frederick., *Estimates and forecasts of extreme poverty by sex and age using the International Futures Model*.

September 2020. Gender-equality-in-the-wake-of-COVID-19-Technical-note-en.pdf (unwomen.org)

[157] UNDP. *COVID-19 will widen the poverty gap between women and men, new UN Women and UNDP data shows*. September 2020 COVID-19 will widen poverty gap between women and men, new UN Women and UNDP data shows | United Nations Development Programme

[158] ditto

[159] M. Savoy, Conor and Staguhn, Janina., *The Role of Water in Catalyzing Gender Equity*. Accessed May 2022. https://www.csis.org/analysis/role-water-catalyzing-gender-equity

[160] Sachetti, Florencia Caro and Petrone, Luciana., *Gender Main streaming in the COVID-19 Policy Response Fostering Equality during the Pandemic and Beyond*, CIPPEC. https://www.cippec.org/wp-content/uploads/2021/05/Global-Solutions-Journal-7-Caro-Sachetti-Petrone.pdf Accessed 15th September 2022

[161] UNDP. SDG 6: *Ensure availability and sustainable management of water and sanitation for all*. Accessed May 2022 https://www.unwomen.org/en/news/in-focus/women-and-the-sdgs/sdg-6-clean-water-sanitation

[162] UNESCO. *Keeping girls in the picture*. Accessed May 2022. https://www.unesco.org/en/covid-19/education-response/keeping-girls-picture

[163] Brownell, Ginanne., *Girls Have Greater Access to Education Than Ever*. Accessed May 2022. https://foreignpolicy.com/2020/10/09/girls-women-education-equality-unesco-global-education-monitoring-report/

[164] Pfunye, Ashlegh and Adempla-Popoola, Iyunoluwa., *The effects of the Covid pandemic on girls' education*. Accessed April 2022 https://www.globalpartnership.org/blog/effects-covid-pandemic-girls-education

[165] Malala Fund. *Malala Fund releases report on girls' education and COVID-19*. Accessed April 2022. https://malala.org/newsroom/malala-fund-releases-report-girls-education-covid-19

[166] Fosci, Mattia., Loffreda, Lucia., Chamberlain, Andrew., Naidoo, Nelisha., *Assessing the needs of the Research System in Ghana*, Research Consulting. HEART. October 2019. https://assets.publishing.service.gov.uk/media/5ef4ac2ad3bf7f7140066006/NA_report_Ghana__Dec_2019_Heart_.pdf. Accessed 7th August 2022

[167] UK Department for International Development. *Assessing the needs of the research system in Ghana: A report for the SRIA programme*, October 2019. Accessed 22 May 2023

[168] Global Innovation Index 2021: *Malaysia*. World Intellectual Property Organization (WIPO), United Nations. https://www.wipo.int/edocs/pubdocs/en/wipo_pub_gii_2021/my.pdf Accessed 7th August

[169] Lawrence, Ruth., *Exploring gender inequity in the context of COVID-19*, KPMG https://home.kpmg/xx/en/home/insights/2021/06/gender-lens-investing.html

[170] UNICEF Ghana. *Girls' Education*, https://www.unicef.org/ghana/girls-education. Accessed 2nd September 2022

[171] Neltoft, C.L., *Girls' education in Ghana: Fighting barriers beyond gender parity*; Global Partnership for Education, October 2021

[172] Mohan, Megha, *'As A Black Woman In STEM I'm Used For Photo Opportunities'*, BBC News. January 2021. https://www.bbc.com/news/business-59897898

[173] Cabell, Autumn., *The Pandemic Is Our Chance to Fix the Black Women in STEM Gap*, Ms Magazine. February 2022. https://msmagazine.com/2022/02/16/Black-women-stem-gap/ Accessed 15th September 2022

[174] Fry, Richard., Kennedy, Brian., and Funk, Cary., *STEM Jobs See Uneven Progress in Increasing Gender, Racial and Ethnic Diversity*. Pew Research Centre. April 2021. https://www.pewresearch.org/science/2021/04/01/stem-jobs-see-uneven-progress-in-increasing-gender-racial-and-ethnic-diversity/ Accessed 4th September 2022

[175] ditto

[176] UK Government. 2 DCMS (2021) *Digital Regulation: Driving growth and unlocking innovation*: https://www.gov.uk/government/publications/digital-regulationdriving-growth-and-unlocking-innovation. Cited April 2023

www.ingramcontent.com/pod-product-compliance
Lightning Source LLC
Chambersburg PA
CBHW070228180526
45158CB00001BA/166